AI in Education: Teaching the Machines to Teach

GoodMan, Volume 1

Patrick Mukosha

Published by Patrick Mukosha, 2025.

AI IN EDUCATION: TEACHING THE MACHINES TO TEACH

First edition. September 7, 2025.

ISBN: 979-8232550677

Written by Patrick Mukosha.

Table of Contents

AI in Education:
Teaching the Machines to Teach

Personalised learning, intelligent tutoring, grading automation, and curriculum design.

•

Copyright Notice

First published: August, 2025

Publisher: Dr Patrick Mukosha

Trademarks

All terms mentioned in this book that are known to be trademarks or service marks have been appropriately capitalized. The Author and the publisher cannot attest to the accuracy of this information. Use of a term in this book should not be regarded as affecting the validity of any trademark or service mark.

Warning and Disclaimer

Every effort has been made to make this book as complete and as accurate as possible, but no warranty or fitness is implied. The information provided in this book is on as is basis. The Author and the Publisher shall have neither liability nor responsibility to any person or entity with respect to any loss or damage arising from the use the information contained in this book.

Author: Patrick Mukosha PhD

Abstract

AI in Education: Teaching the Machines to Teach examines how 21st-century classrooms, teachers, and students are changing as a result of artificial intelligence. In order to demonstrate how technology might serve as a co-teacher rather than a substitute for human educators, the book examines the transition from traditional content distribution to personalized, adaptive learning systems driven by AI.

It addresses the issues of prejudice, data privacy, and an excessive dependence on algorithms while highlighting the potential of AI—from real-time language translation and intelligent tutoring systems to predictive analytics that promote student success—by drawing on case studies from around the world.

The book's core contention is that, in an AI-driven society, educators continue to be indispensable not only as knowledge brokers but also as mentors, emotional support systems, and moral advisors.

In the end, AI in Education advocates for a rethinking of education in which robots and humans co-evolve. *In a world where technology and mankind must coexist, it exhorts legislators, educators, and students to embrace AI responsibly in order to prepare future generations for a lifetime of learning.*

Chapter 1: The Development of Education: From Whiteboards to Algorithms

Overview: Educational Methods throughout History

The foundation of human advancement has always been education. *Teaching has continuously changed to satisfy society demands, starting with the earliest times when knowledge was transmitted orally in tribal assemblies and continuing through the founding of institutional institutions in ancient Greece, Rome, and China.* The chalkboard has represented organized, group learning for millennia. It changed classrooms by allowing teachers to teach topics to large groups of students at once when it was first introduced in the early 19th century.

During the chalkboard period, pupils copied information and repeated lessons, emphasizing rote learning and memory. Later, the industrial-style classroom—rows of desks, a single teacher, and a standardized curriculum intended to shape pupils into uniform workers for an industrial economy—emerged as printed textbooks made standardized knowledge more accessible to all.

Although effective, *this technique had trouble accommodating individual learning styles.* While faster learners were frequently under-stimulated, students who fell behind seldom received individualized support. Many kids were underserved by the one-size-fits-all approach, which led to a need for instruments and strategies that could scale customisation.

As a result, classrooms in the twenty-first century are drastically changing. Previously dominated by chalk and talk, data, algorithms, and intelligent technologies are now starting to influence how students learn and professors instruct.

Artificial intelligence (AI), which is now incorporated into common educational resources and is subtly "teaching the machines to teach," is no longer limited to science fiction.

AI has started to address long-standing issues in education, such as scalability, inclusivity, and accessibility, through intelligent tutoring systems that serve as virtual teaching assistants and adaptive learning platforms that tailor training for each student.

The innovations, difficulties, and possibilities in this new field are examined in this book.

1.1. Computers and E-Learning Platforms' Introduction

The introduction of computers into classrooms in the latter half of the 20th century marked a sea change. Early educational software like as LOGO, Reader Rabbit, and Math Blaster brought interactive learning to classrooms in the 1980s and 1990s. With the help of practice questions, tests, and basic animations, these apps enhanced the learning experience.

Using phrases like "computer-aided instruction," "blended instruction," and "personalized learning," for instance, the boundaries between the roles of teachers and computers have been debated in education for decades. However, how are decisions about instruction determined in systems that combine algorithms and humans?

AI tools and systems are already making it possible to modify lesson plans to meet the needs of students in order to provide them with feedback and pointers, such as when they are completing arithmetic problems or learning a foreign language. With the increasing capabilities and widespread usage of AI-enabled systems and applications, this conversation over the application of AI in classroom pedagogy and student learning will be reinvigorated and intensified.

E-learning was propelled by the internet by the early 2000s. Students could access classes and assignments from any location, and teachers could publish course materials online thanks to platforms like Moodle and Blackboard. The Learning Management System (LMS) era began with this change, and digital platforms became crucial to education.

E-learning provided a number of benefits:

- **Accessibility:** By removing geographical restrictions, students could learn remotely.
- **Scalability:** Thousands of students could enrol in a single

course.

- **Flexibility:** Students could access the material at any time and learn at their own speed.

These platforms did, however, still mostly mimic conventional techniques. Although digital, the content was not always customized. Regardless of skill level, students absorbed the same information, mirroring the classroom's homogeneity—this time via screens.

1.2. What Sets the Leap into AI Apart from Conventional EdTech

The introduction of artificial intelligence (AI) into the classroom signified a paradigm shift rather than merely the digitization of instruction. AI systems adapt to learners, in contrast to e-learning platforms that merely delivered content.

What distinguishes AI?

1. Scalable Personalization

AI examines information from each learner's interactions, including how quickly they respond, where they make mistakes, and which subjects they are best at, and then adjusts the content accordingly. This enables personalized learning pathways that were previously unattainable in big classrooms.

2. Real-Time Feedback

In traditional schooling, feedback is postponed until instructor reviews or tests. AI instructors give pupils immediate feedback so they may fix errors right away.

3. Administrative Task Automation

Teachers can concentrate on mentorship and creative involvement as AI takes care of grading, attendance monitoring, and even curriculum modifications.

4. The Ability To Make Predictions

AI can determine if a pupil is going to struggle or succeed by evaluating performance data, enabling early interventions.

With this advancement, AI is no longer just a tool but an intelligent collaborator in education, revolutionizing both teaching and learning.

1.3. Case Study: Khan Academy's Ascent and How It Prepared the Way for AI Tutors

The Khan Academy tale serves as an example of how technology made AI-driven education possible. Salman Khan launched the website in 2008 with basic YouTube math lessons. It developed into a global centre for e-learning over time, providing teacher dashboards, interactive exercises, and free video classes.

Important developments that paved the way for AI tutors:

- **Self-Paced Learning:** As a first step toward personalized learning, students could pause, fast-forward, and review lessons until they understand.
- **Data Tracking**: Before AI's analytics-driven customisation, progress dashboards gave teachers and students the ability to track their strengths and shortcomings.
- **Scalability:** Digital platforms have the ability to democratize education, as demonstrated by the fact that one teacher, Sal Khan, was able to reach millions of students.

Even if Khan Academy is not entirely AI-powered, it did show how much demand there is for individualized, flexible education. Its popularity sparked the creation of AI tutors that could customize courses for every learner, transforming static films into intelligent, interactive learning partners.

Final Thoughts

The transition from chalkboards to algorithms illustrates how education is always changing. Oral tradition, chalkboards, printed textbooks, e-learning, and now artificial intelligence have all changed how people learn and increased access.

AI signifies the biggest change to date: a move from mass education to large-scale individualized intelligence. AI promises to comprehend and react to each learner as an individual, much as chalkboards brought schools together and e-learning connected the world.

Therefore, human-AI collaboration—teachers as mentors and guides, backed by intelligent systems that adapt, scale, and improve the learning experience for every student—is more important for the future of teaching than technology alone.

1.4. Other Mini-Case Studies: Adaptive AI vs. Static Platforms

1.4.1. Personalized Language Learning with Duolingo's AI Tutor

With more than 500 million users since its 2011 start, Duolingo has grown to become one of the most popular language-learning websites worldwide. Its secret is AI-driven personalization as well as gamification.

- **Adaptive Lessons:** The system modifies lessons in real time based on individual learner's vocabulary, grammatical errors, and response speeds.
- **Spaced Repetition**: AI determines when a student is most likely to lose a phrase or idea and reinforces retention by returning it at the right times.
- **Gamification with Intelligence:** Duolingo's AI challenges students at the ideal level of difficulty to maintain motivation in place of static exercises.

Duolingo demonstrates how artificial intelligence (AI) can personalize mass learning, guaranteeing that each student advances at their own speed while retaining interest.

1.4.2. AI in Math Education at Carnegie Learning

Early in the new millennium, Carnegie Learning, which grew out of cognitive science research at Carnegie Mellon University, invented AI-based math tutoring programs. Their platform, MATHia, simulates how children learn mathematics by using cognitive models:

- **Step-by-Step Guidance**: AI examines every step a student takes to solve an issue rather than just rating responses as correct or incorrect.
- **Error Diagnosis:** The program recognizes common misconceptions (such misinterpreting fractions) and provides tailored solutions.
- **Support for Teachers**: AI dashboards emphasize the subjects that students find most difficult to understand, enabling teachers to modify their lesson plans.

This example demonstrates how AI can enhance teachers rather than replace them by offering profound insights into student performance.

1.5. Using ChatGPT as a Conversational AI Learning Aid in Classrooms

The emergence of massive language models such as ChatGPT has created completely new opportunities. ChatGPT is capable of having organic, lively discussions with students in a variety of subjects, in contrast to pre-programmed teaching systems:

- **On-Demand Tutoring:** Students can ask questions at any moment and get individualized, straightforward explanations.
- **Various Viewpoints:** Depending on the demands of the students, the AI can convey the same idea in a variety of methods, including visual, step-by-step, and analogy-based.
- **Creative Collaboration:** In addition to academics, students utilize ChatGPT to practice debates, develop essay topics, and even role-play historical personalities for a more in-depth experience.

ChatGPT shows the transition from structured tutoring systems to open-ended, conversational learning partners—something traditional EdTech never accomplished—even though issues with accuracy and ethical use still exist.

1.5.1. Connecting the Evolution

Why Khan Academy remained stagnant while making knowledge widely available:

- **Duolingo and Carnegie Learning:** Adaptive AI was launched by Duolingo and Carnegie Learning, which allows content to be tailored to learner performance. ChatGPT is the first step toward general-purpose AI tutoring, in which the computer mimics a human tutor by conversing and delivering lessons.

This trajectory demonstrates the evolution of education from material distribution to personalization to intelligent interaction, laying the groundwork for a time when AI tutors will be commonplace learning partners.

1.6. A Look at the Future: The Classroom Driven by AI

Picture yourself entering a school in 2035. The instructor remains at the forefront, but not as a lecturer but rather as a learning architect who directs the flow of information. Students are gathered around them, each interacting with their AI learning partner.

Every student's AI teacher discreetly modifies lessons in real time on a wearable headset or digital tablet. While a student who excels in mathematics faces difficulties with early calculus, another who struggles with algebra receives step-by-step issue breakdowns. The AI is aware of their advantages, disadvantages, and even preferred method of learning, be it gamified challenges, real-world applications, or visual diagrams.

A comprehensive picture of the class, including who is succeeding, who is behind, and which ideas require group reinforcement, is displayed on the teacher's AI dashboard in the meantime. The teacher prioritizes mentoring, creativity, and emotional intelligence—areas where human connection is most important—instead of spending hours marking papers.

The classroom is more than just its walls. Under the guidance of their AI instructors, who effortlessly translate languages and suggest materials appropriate for their cultural backgrounds, a child in Zambia works in real time on a science project with a peer in Japan. Age, location, and strict schedules are no longer barriers to education, which becomes global, individualized, and ongoing.

This isn't science fiction; rather, it's the natural progression from chalkboards to Khan Academy and, more recently, AI-powered friends like ChatGPT, MATHia, and Duolingo.

Learning was originally unified by the chalkboard. Platforms for e-learning made it global. However, artificial intelligence (AI) promises to humanize it, making sure that learning eventually fits the learner rather than the other way around.

Chapter 2: Tailored Education: Each Learner, Their Own Journey

Overview

The foundation of education has always been the development of the individual student, although traditional classroom settings frequently fall short of this ideal. *It is not feasible for a teacher with forty students to create forty distinct lesson plans each day.* The outcome? While some students silently lag behind, others sprint ahead.

This equation is being altered by artificial intelligence. *Personalized learning is now a reality because to sophisticated algorithms, flexible platforms, and real-time feedback.* Every learner can now pursue a personalized educational path that is suited to their strengths and weaknesses, independent of pace, learning style, or background.

One question becomes crucial as we enter this new era: *What function do human teachers serve if AI is capable of teaching?* The reimagined role of educators at a time when machines can tutor, grade, and even create curricula will be discussed in Chapter 2, but they will never be able to fully replace the distinctively human traits of inspiration, empathy, and wisdom.

2.1. How AI Modifies Instruction to Fit Different Learning Styles and Paces

Large volumes of student data are gathered and analysed by AI-powered learning systems, including quiz results, response times, preferred learning forms (text, video, interactive simulation), and even behavioural indicators like hesitation or recurrent errors. The system makes real-time adjustments based on this:

- **Adaptive Pacing:** The AI can advance to more complex subjects if a student swiftly solves algebraic problems. It offers more step-by-step instructions and support for slower learners.
- **Various Modalities**: While some students learn well with visual assistance, others benefit more from storytelling or practical experience. AI systems can change formats to accommodate different learning styles.
- **Continuous Assessment**: AI continuously assesses performance rather than waiting for midterm exams, guaranteeing that misunderstandings are cleared up right away rather than months later.

The conventional "one-size-fits-all" classroom is changed into a "many-paths-for-many-minds" environment by this innovative method.

2.1.1. American DreamBox Learning

For pupils in grades K–8, DreamBox is an adaptive math program. It keeps note of each click, pause, and problem-solving attempt, using this information to instantaneously modify the lesson's complexity. A confident student may be presented with word problems that require critical thinking, whereas a child who struggles with fractions may be given visual aids and detailed explanations.

2.1.2. The Australian Smart Sparrow

Higher education was the target market for this flexible e-learning platform. Depending on how students respond, professors can design courses with branching pathways that let them go through the content in multiple ways. Instead of just marking a virtual patient incorrectly, Smart Sparrow offers guidance, reroutes the student back through anatomical basics, and re-presents the case until mastery is attained.

2.1.3. Kenya's Eneza Education

Eneza Education has used low-tech mobile phones to provide AI-powered individualized tutoring in areas with restricted access to high-tech gadgets. Students receive tailored lectures in core subjects, quizzes, and feedback via SMS and simple internet-enabled devices. In rural Africa, where typical teacher-to-student ratios often reach 1:60, this low-cost strategy is revolutionizing education.

2.2. AI Facilitates Learning Adaptability

One important way that technology can enhance learning is through adaptability. AI can be used as a toolkit to increase edtech's adaptability. *The ability of a technology to meet students where they are, build on their strengths, and expand their knowledge and abilities may be enhanced by artificial intelligence.*

AI can be a particularly powerful toolkit for increasing the adaptability offered to students due to its ability to deal with natural forms of input and the fundamental characteristics of AI models.

However, adaptivity is always more focused and specialized than what a general term like "meet students where they are" could imply, particularly when it comes to AI. The nature of the model at the core of any given AI-enabled system gives rise to core limitations. Approximations of reality are what models are.

The resulting adaptivity will also be limited, and the learning supports may be fragile or narrow, when significant aspects of human learning are excluded from the model or are not completely developed. As a result, the main idea of this section on learning is: Aim for AI models that encompass all learning visions; do not confine learning to what AI is now capable of accurately simulating.

Thanks to developments in what are known as "large language models" or occasionally "foundational models," AI models are exhibiting increased proficiency. There are some limitations to even extremely broad models. For instance, generative AI models shown in the media may produce persuasive essays on a wide range of subjects in a short amount of time, but other models can produce believable pictures with only a few suggestions.

Experts in our listening sessions cautioned that, despite the enthusiasm surrounding foundational models, AI models are more limited than human learning visions, and that it is still crucial to build learning environments with these constraints in mind. Additionally, the models are fragile and perform poorly in changing circumstances. They also lack the same "common sense" judgment as people, which frequently results in them reacting in strange or inappropriate ways. Considering the surprising ways that foundational models fall short, it is nevertheless crucial to keep humans informed.

2.3. Advantages of AI-Powered Personalized Learning

- **Lowering the Rate of Dropouts** :

Because the curriculum either goes too quickly, leaving them lost, or too slowly, leaving them bored, many students leave out. This gap is filled by personalized learning, which maintains each student's level of engagement.

- **Improving Exam Results**:

Adaptive learning guarantees mastery prior to advancement. Students perform more consistently and are better prepared for tests when learning gaps are filled right away. According to studies, students who use AI-powered resources like DreamBox outperform their counterparts in traditional settings in math by up to 60%.

- **Encouraging Equity:**

AI has no discrimination. The system offers continuous attention, individualized advice, and resources that are in line with the needs of every child, regardless of whether they reside in Silicon Valley or a small Kenyan town.

Diagram: AI-Powered Personalised Learning

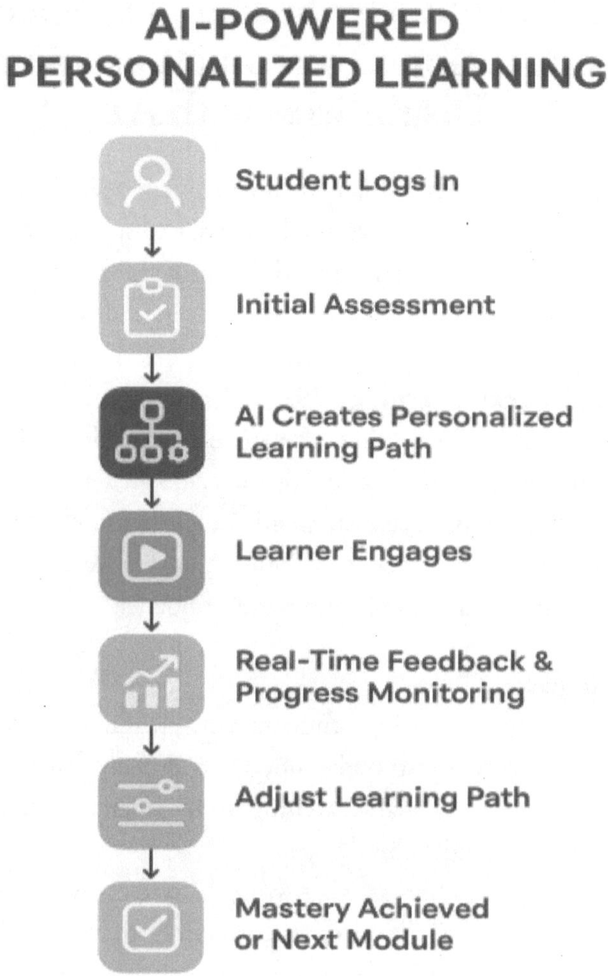

Figure 1: AI-Powered Personalised Learning

2.3. Case Study: Students in Special Education Overcome Learning Disabilities with AI

The range of demands, which includes autism spectrum disorders, dyslexia, and ADHD, has presented a barrier to special education for many years. The resources needed to provide these pupils with customized attention were sometimes lacking in traditional classrooms. These days, AI is changing the game.

Example: Lexia Learning (USA)

AI is used in Lexia's reading software to assist dyslexic kids. It offers focused activities and breaks reading down into micro-skills (phonemic awareness, vocabulary, and comprehension). The software changes focus to strengthen that foundation before continuing if a pupil has trouble with letter-sound correspondence.

- **Impact:**
    - Lexia-using students with reading problems have demonstrated notable literacy improvements, occasionally catching up by several grade levels in a single school year.
    - Teachers say that while AI systems take care of basic practice and error correction, they can concentrate on higher-level support, such as emotional support, confidence development, and one-on-one coaching.
- **Beyond Literacy**: AI-powered voice recognition software is helping pupils who are nonverbal by deciphering gestures and vocalization efforts and converting them into speech or text. AI-powered social simulations give autistic kids a secure way to practice real-world interactions while boosting their social confidence.

In conclusion, AI-powered personalized learning aims to unleash human potential rather than merely raise test scores. AI is changing the educational landscape by allowing each student to follow their own path. There is a noticeable change from university lecture halls to special education programs, and from math classrooms in the US to rural schools in Kenya, the future of education is mass personalization rather than mass instruction.

Diagram: Visual Aid: Advantages of AI-Powered Personalised Learning Flowchart

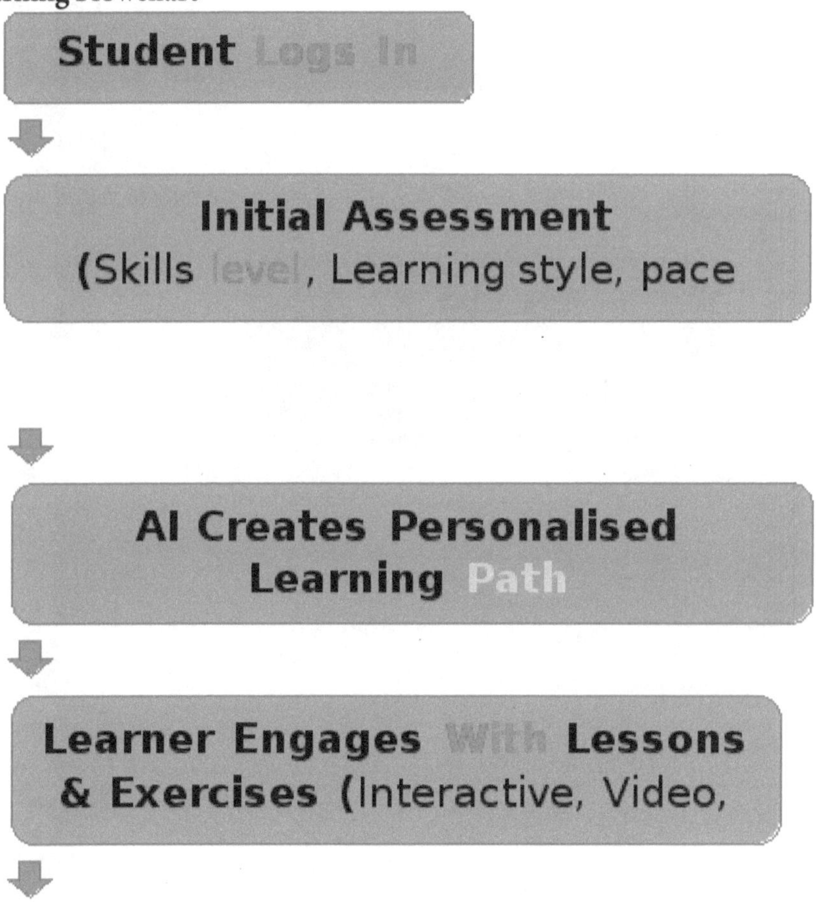

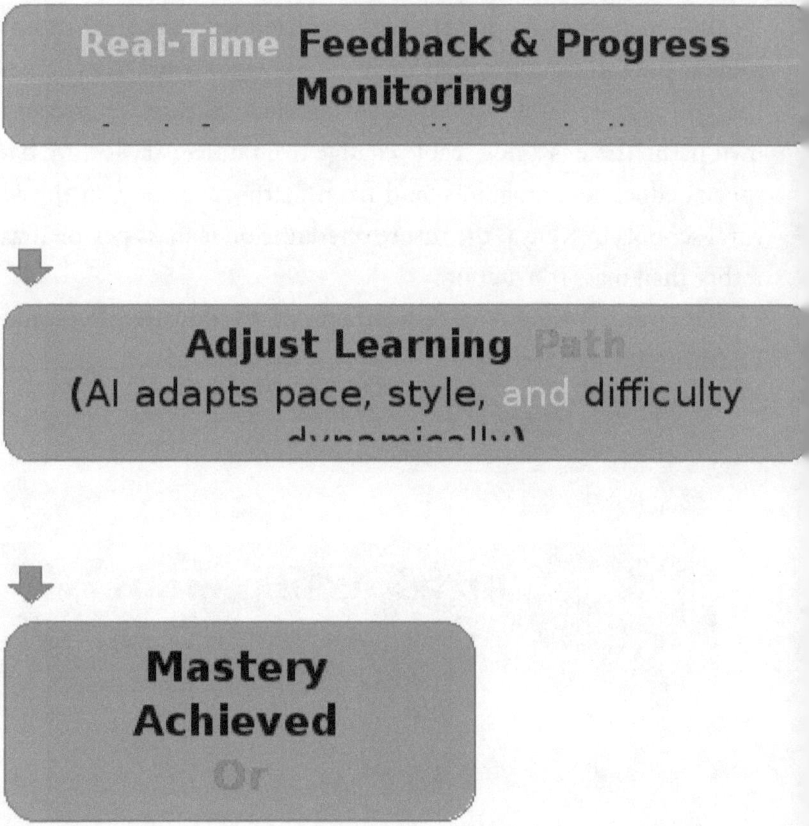
Real-Time Feedback & Progress
Monitoring
Adjust Learning Path
(AI adapts pace, style, and difficulty
Mastery
Achieved
Or

Figure 2: Visual Aid: Advantages of AI-Powered Personalised Learning Flowchart

Chapter 3: Intelligent Tutoring Systems: The Digital Instructor That Is Always There

***AI Tutors** provide one-on-one teaching at any time and from any location by talking, diagnosing, and adapting* - Patrick Mukosha.

3.1. Intelligent Tutoring Systems (ITS): What Are They?

An Intelligent Tutoring System (ITS) is one of the most established forms of AI-enabled technology. Scientists were able to create precise models of how human specialists resolve mathematical issues in an early success. The final model was integrated into a system that would track students' problem-solving while they worked on computer-based mathematics issues.

Researchers who looked at human tutors discovered that one of the main reasons tutoring works so well is probably because it provides feedback on individual steps rather than just correct or wrong answers.

When a student deviated from the expert model, for instance, the system provided feedback to assist the learner in reorienting themselves. Crucially, the model was able to offer feedback on certain parts of a solution process rather than just good or wrong. Therefore, the ability of AI to provide adaptivity at the step-by-step level and to do so at scale with a moderate cost can be considered a significant achievement.

Thus, AI-powered learning platforms called Intelligent Tutoring Systems (ITS) are made to offer individualized, flexible instruction. In contrast to static e-learning platforms, ITS provides feedback, recommendations, and customized learning routes based on the learner's understanding.

The effort has expanded beyond mathematical difficulties to other significant concerns outside methodical problem solving as a research and development (R&D) field has arisen to promote ITS. There are certain restrictions in the early work. An ITS could handle closed tasks that were mathematical or logical in nature, with explicit requirements for the nature of the solution and the solution method.

Additionally, early AI models' "approximation of reality" was focused on cognition rather than other facets of human learning, such social or motivational factors. These early restrictions have since been addressed in two ways: by enlarging AI models and by including people into the process, which is also a crucial viewpoint today.

Today, for instance, a human instructor could still be in charge of encouraging student participation and self-regulation in addition to other areas of instruction if an ITS focuses on feedback as a student practice. In other modern instances, teachers deal with pupils in small groups while the computer ITS focuses on problem-solving exercises.

Additionally, students can be involved with AI using "open learner models," a kind of AI-enabled system that offers data to encourage students' introspection and self-monitoring.

Essential Elements of ITS:

- **Domain Model:** Describes the subject knowledge, including required relationships, rules, concepts, and techniques for solving problems.
- **Student Model:** Monitors learners' progress, knowledge, and misconceptions in real time. Employs methods such as Deep Knowledge Tracing and Bayesian Knowledge Tracing.
- **Pedagogical Model**: Chooses when to offer clarifications, tips, or extra exercises as educational tactics.
- **Interface Layer:** Provides teachers with interactive exercises, voice, chat, and dashboards.
- **Data & Analytics**: Facilitates ongoing system enhancement by tracking student performance, engagement, and retention.

3.2. A Duality: Acquiring Knowledge About and Using AI

Two main viewpoints on AI in education emerge as it is introduced into classrooms: (1) AI to enhance student learning, and (2) support for education on AI and associated technologies. Thus far, we have talked about AI tools and systems that help students learn and become proficient in disciplines like writing and mathematics.

However, it's equally crucial that students study artificial intelligence (AI), analyse its use in society and education, and assess its worth and function in their own lives and careers. In this report, we address hazards in every part.

Since AI is present in every aspect of students' life, it is crucial that they become more knowledgeable of and sensitive to its risks, which include those of bias and surveillance. For instance, schools have recently assisted students in comprehending cybersecurity. Students need to be aware of the new threats that artificial intelligence will bring. We're inspired by initiatives that we've seen in progress that would allow students to study AI's operation while also having a conversation on pertinent subjects like security and privacy.

As we've seen, elementary, middle, and high school kids can start studying about artificial intelligence. They can employ AI to create products and simulations that excite them. Additionally, we've observed that students have a lot to say about the kinds of items they'd want to see in schools and want to discuss the ethics of the things they use on a daily basis.

The demand for co-design approaches that involve students in developing the future generation of AI-enabled edtech is also mentioned later in the book. In general, it's critical to strike a balance between providing students with opportunity to learn about AI and focusing on using AI to enhance learning.

3.3. Tutoring with Natural Language Processing (NLP)

The interaction engine of ITS is natural language processing (NLP), which allows the system to comprehend, interpret, and reply to students in natural language.

Important ITS NLP Functions:

1. **Intent Recognition:** Determines if a pupil is posing a query, resolving an issue, or looking for clarification.

2. **Semantic Parsing:** To verify accuracy and spot misunderstandings, this method transforms free-text responses into structured representations.

3. **Using progressive cues**—questions → scaffolds → worked examples—Socratic prompting helps students.

4. **Error Detection & Feedback**: Recognizes misunderstandings and offers focused remedial advice.

5. **Dialogue Management**: Preserves context throughout various exchanges to guarantee training that makes sense.

6. **Metacognitive Coaching**: Enhances long-term learning by promoting introspection and self-explanation.

7. **Speech and Multilingual Support**: Facilitates accessibility and native language instruction.

Dialogue Example:

- **Learner:** "I calculated -3x + 5 = 11." I believe that x equals 2.

- **Tutor:** "Well done! How should we use the +5?
- **Learner:** "Subtract 5 from both sides."
- **Tutor:** "That's right. Thus, -3x = 6. Now find x.
- **Learner:** "x = -2."
- **Tutor:** "Great! Keep in mind that while dividing both sides by -3 maintains equality, it modifies the sign consideration for inequality.

3.4. Error and Adaptive Questioning Making a diagnosis

By adjusting the material and level of difficulty to each student's proficiency, adaptive questioning maximizes learning outcomes and student engagement.

Methods:

- **Item Response Theory (IRT):** Assigns a student's estimated skill to the complexity of the assignment.
- **Knowledge Tracing (BKT/DKT):** Real-time updates of each concept's mastery probability.
- **Reinforcement Learning**: Chooses the best teaching strategy to maximize long-term learning outcomes.
- **Error Diagnosis**: Provides accurate, customized feedback by utilizing misperception libraries and signature error detection.

Simplified Adaptive Loop Example:

1. Choose an idea by looking at the student model.
2. Identify an issue.
3. Examine the answer.
4. Make changes to the student model.
5. If necessary, offer focused remediation.
6. Set up a review or go on to the following idea.

3.4. Crucial Paths to Advance AI-Based Adaptibility

"Personalization" is another term for adaptability. Many commentators have pointed out how ambiguous this term is, despite its convenience. Giving students "voice and choice" is one way that some educators define customization, while others define it as having a learning management system suggest a unique "playlist" of activities for every student.

The fact that many edtech devices that offer personalization only do so in a few ways is concealed within that imprecision. One of the two most popular ways that edtech products adapt is by changing the course materials' order and level of difficulty. However, any educator is aware that enhancing learning involves more than merely changing the level of difficulty and order of the materials.

An effective teacher can, for instance, use personal experiences to interest a student and can mold explanations until they truly resonate and the learner has a "aha!" moment. Compared to the majority of edtech, human teachers provide a far more comprehensive picture of each learner when we say, "meet the learner where they are."

Additionally, the instructor is unlikely to "over-personalise"—that is, act as an algorithm that only shows content that the student has indicated interest in—which would limit the student's exposure to novel subjects. A human teacher's understanding of "teachable moments" is more expansive than that of today's AI models.

3.5. Creating, Choosing and Assessing AI Tools

The loop that decides which resources are available and what they do in the classroom is the most comprehensive one in which teachers should participate. Teachers are already involved in the design and selection of technologies nowadays. Teachers can comment on practicality and usability. Teachers discuss their results with other school administrators after reviewing efficacy evidence. Teachers already exchange ideas about how to effectively use technology.

- These worries go beyond data security and privacy; they draw attention to the ways in which technologies may unjustly restrict or guide some kids' educational opportunities.
- These worries will persist, but AI will also give rise to new ones. The Formative Assessment portion that follows, for instance, presents questions regarding fairness and prejudice that may result in algorithmic discrimination.
- One important conclusion from this is that in order for teachers to fully engage in risk-reduction design, selection, and evaluation procedures, they will require time and assistance to stay up to date on both well-known and emerging topics.

3.6. Top Intelligent Learning Platforms

1. **(MATHia) Carnegie Learning**

- **Emphasis:** Mathematics in middle and high schools.
- **Advantages:** Teacher dashboards, mastery monitoring, and step-level feedback.
- **Use:** Blended learning, which frees up teachers to concentrate on teaching in small groups.

1. **Squirrel** AI

- **Emphasis:** Language, science, and math adaptive tutoring.
- **Advantages:** Tailored learning pathways, scalable centres, and fine-grained diagnostics.
- **Use:** Especially successful in underprivileged communities where there is a teacher shortage.

1. **IBM Watson Tutor**

- **Emphasis:** Natural language tutoring tailored to a particular domain.
- **Advantages**: retrieval-augmented responses, NLP-driven explanations, and subject-specific adaptability.
- **Use:** Advanced high school courses and enterprise training.

3.7. Case Study: The Effect of Squirrel AI in Rural China

Challenge:

- The challenge Multi-grade classes and a significant teacher shortage are problems in many rural Chinese areas.

Intervention:

- **Diagnostic Assessment:** Every student takes an adaptive test that maps their knowledge across hundreds of micro-skills as part of the diagnostic assessment process.
- **Customized Learning Paths:** ITS organizes exercises, courses, and micro-remediation to fill up specific deficiencies.
- **Oversight of Teachers:** Local facilitators keep an eye on dashboards and only offer assistance when required.
- **Outcome Tracking:** Weekly dashboards track learning progress, hint usage, and student mastery.

Result:

- Using conventional approaches, students below grade level caught up more quickly than their peers.
- Consistent learning quality in spite of the availability of local teachers.
- More educational equity for pupils living in rural areas.

Lessons Learned:

- Mapping knowledge at the granular level is crucial.
- Frequent, brief sessions enhance retention.

- Signals of involvement and motivation must be included.
- Adaptation to language and culture improves efficacy.

3.8. Enhancing Teaching Jobs with AI

Teachers have long imagined a lot of things that technology may do for them, their pupils, and their classrooms, *but they haven't considered the changes brought about by the current pandemic.* Almost all educators today have encountered unexpected applications of technology in the classroom.

There were some good experiences and some bad ones. As we continue to consider teaching with technology, all of the experiences offer a crucial backdrop. It is imperative that the difficulties faced by educators be addressed. Teachers must find it simpler to perform the incredible work they consistently do.

We must also keep in mind the reasons behind people's decision to become teachers and make sure they are capable of performing the important tasks. Examples of AI assisting teachers and teaching are covered in this section, including the following ideas: AI that helps teachers plan, reflect, and enhance their practice; AI that helps teachers make recommendations for their students' needs and extend their work with them; and AI that helps teachers lessen the burden of routine teaching duties.

Teachers have a famously difficult profession because they have to make thousands of judgments every day. Instructors take part in administrative tasks, work with other instructors, engage with students outside of the classroom, and participate in classroom procedures. They are required to engage with families and caregivers because they are also a part of their communities.

We consider how much simpler some daily chores have gotten. We are able to send and receive event alerts and notifications. Even with digital music, choosing the music we want to listen to use to require a number of steps. However, these days, we can simply say the name of a song we want to hear, and it will start playing.

Similarly, planning a trip used to involve a laborious review of maps, but now days, cell phones enable us to select from a variety of modes of transportation to get to our destination:

- *Why shouldn't the resources available to teachers help them quickly adjust to the needs and strengths of their students as things in the classroom change, as they always do?*
- *Why can't educators be given the tools they need to implement a technology-rich lesson plan and the assistance they need to recognize the evolving requirements of their students?*
- *Why is it so difficult for them to arrange the learning paths of their students?*

3.9. School Integration Models

1. Station Rotation: As professors conduct lessons, students move between ITS stations for practice.

2. Flipped Classroom: Projects and discussions take place in class while students do the ITS modules at home.

3. Acceleration Labs: Intense ITS-based instruction for fast-tracking or remediation.

4. Homework Companion: ITS offers immediate assistance with homework.

3.7. Governance, Equity, and Ethics

- Make sure the material is inclusive and equitable.
- Adhere to regional laws regarding data security and privacy.
- To address complicated misconceptions and socio-emotional assistance, keep human teachers informed.
- Make system decisions and feedback transparent.

3.8. AI Systems Open Up New Ways to Communicate

Artificial intelligence (AI) models enable computational processes to support more natural types of contact, such talking to an assistant, and to make suggestions or plans. The potential of AI-enabled educational systems to facilitate more organic interactions during instruction will contribute to their desirability.

There are few methods for teachers and students to engage with edtech on traditional edtech sites:

- In a multiple-choice question or from a menu, teachers and students can select options.
- They might type brief responses.
- They might use touch gestures or drag items around the screen.
- Teachers and students receive outputs from the computer in the form of multimedia, text, and images.

Despite the versatility of various input and output formats, this type of interaction is unique to human-computer interaction and cannot be confused with two humans interacting with each other. AI is expected to make computer-human interactions more akin to one another. An AI assistant may respond when a teacher speaks to it. A section of a drawing created by a student might be highlighted by the computer.

Similar to how modern email systems can finish ideas faster than humans can type them, a teacher or student may begin writing something and the computer may finish their phrase.

Furthermore, there is a growing range of automated operations that AI systems can perform. Present-day personalization systems have the ability to automatically modify the learning sessions' pace, sequence, cues, or trajectory. Future initiatives may include an AI tool or system that assists students with their homework or a teaching assistant that lightens the effort of teachers by suggesting lesson plans that meet their needs and are comparable to those they have appreciated in the past.

Additionally, in a small group of students working on a collaborative task, an AI-enabled assistance might show up as an extra "partner." Complex classroom routines may also benefit from the assistance of an AI-enabled technology.

3.9. Future Paths

- **Multimodal Tutors:** Combine interactive tools, speech, text, and simulations.
- **Profiles of Lifelong Learners**: Maintain misconceptions and knowledge over years and subjects.
- **Teacher-Authorable AI:** Give educators the ability to design and modify ITS materials.
- **On-Device Tutoring:** Low-latency, privacy-preserving ITS solutions on nearby devices.

Diagram: Intelligent Tutoring System

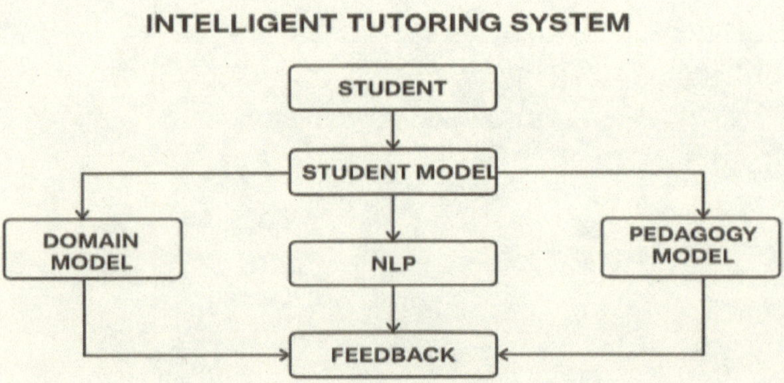

Figure 3: Intelligent Tutoring System

Note: This chapter highlights how ITS uses natural language processing (NLP), adaptive learning, and human supervision to function as a digital instructor around-the-clock, enabling scalable, individualized, and high-quality teaching.

3.10. A Problem: Considering AI in Education from a Systems Perspective

Participants in our listening session reminded us that as AI becomes more prevalent in the educational system, it will be integrating into currently broken areas or sections of the system. AI must be employed even more carefully in situations where the context of the systems is unstable or unpredictable; it is by no means a solution to damaged systems.

As was previously mentioned, we must create educational environments that place AI in a way that allows teachers and other adults to effectively use these technologies for teaching and learning because AI systems and tools do not entirely match learning objectives.

The ITS example demonstrated how AI may improve the effectiveness of math problem practice, and a comprehensive curriculum approach could involve teaching roles that prioritize mathematical techniques like modelling and reasoning. Additionally, small-group work is probably going to continue to be significant: *While working in small groups to answer to a realistic situation, students may apply mathematics to forecast or justify.*

Understanding how learning can be culturally responsive and culturally sustaining is now the "right place" for people, not AI, as AI is still far from being prepared to link learning to the distinctive qualities in a student's family and culture.

3.11. Key Recommendations: Look For AI Models That Support A Learning Vision.

We've highlighted how adaptivity is impacted by AI advancements, but we've also highlighted how adaptivity is constrained by the intrinsic qualities of the model. We saw that the term "personalized" was employed differently in a previous wave of edtech, and that it was frequently necessary to define what personalization meant for a certain good or service. Therefore, our main suggestion is to concentrate on AI models that closely match desired learning visions and to test the capabilities and limitations of AI models in upcoming edtech products.

Since artificial intelligence is developing quickly these days, we need distinguish between products with basic AI-like capabilities and those with more complex AI models. There is a noticeable push and effort being made to overcome these constraints when we look at what is occurring in research and development. We pointed out that since there is no such thing as generic artificial intelligence, decision makers should exercise caution when choosing AI models that could limit their capacity for learning.

Furthermore, since AI models can never be as comprehensive as real-world experience, we must go forward with systems thinking that involves humans and takes into account the advantages and disadvantages of the particular educational system. We maintain that the learning system as a whole is more comprehensive than just its AI component.

Chapter 4: Eliminating Red Tape for Teachers with Grading Automation

Overview

One of the most tedious and time-consuming duties teachers have to perform is grading. The development of artificial intelligence (AI) has given teachers the ability to automate grading, which improves uniformity, speeds up feedback, and frees up critical time for deeper student engagement. This chapter examines how artificial intelligence (AI) is changing grading procedures, emphasizing both objective and subjective evaluations. Notable resources such as Gradescope and Turnitin's e-rater are highlighted, along with the advantages they offer educational environments.

Diagram: Grading Automation

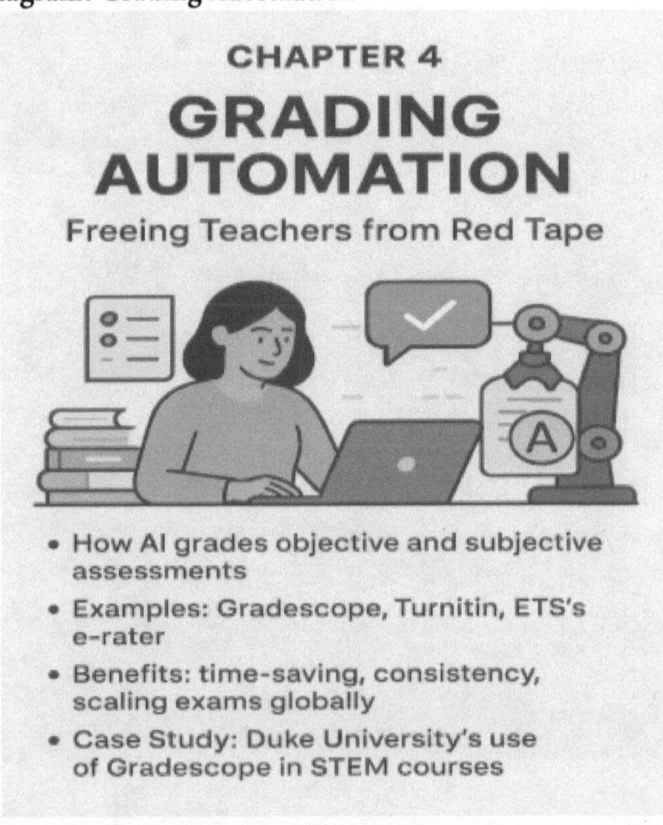

Figure 4: Grading Automation - Freeing Teachers from Red Tape

4.1. Grading using AI: Objective and Subjective Evaluations

4.1.1. Objective Evaluations

AI systems can easily grade objective tests like multiple-choice questions (MCQs), true/false questions, and fill-in-the-blank questions. AI can assess these answers fast, giving pupils feedback right away and relieving teachers of some of the grading duties.

4.1.2. Subjective Evaluations

Because they are more open-ended, subjective tests—such as essays, short answers, and coding assignments—present a bigger difficulty. Advanced natural language processing (NLP) and machine learning methods are used by AI systems such as Gradescope and Turnitin's e-rater to evaluate these responses. To produce consistent and impartial assessments, these tools examine elements including grammar, coherence, logic, and relevance.

4.2. Prominent AI Grading Resources

4.2.1. Gradescope

Handwritten, multiple-choice, and programming assignments are among the assessment modalities supported by Gradescope, an AI-powered grading platform. By combining related responses into groups and using the same criteria for all entries, it enables teachers to assess assignments quickly. Grading time is greatly decreased by the platform's AI-assisted grading feature, which rapidly finds and grades comparable responses.

4.2.2. The e-rater on Turnitin

An AI-powered technology called Turnitin's e-rater is used to evaluate writing skills. It assesses writings according to their organization, style, mechanics, language, and usage. Students receive immediate feedback from the e-rater, which helps them hone their writing abilities before to final submission. Additionally, it helps teachers by pointing out areas where students frequently make mistakes, allowing for more focused instructional interventions.

4.2.3. The e-rater of ETS

The e-rater scoring engine, provided by the Educational Testing Service (ETS), automatically grades essays and offers writing criticism. By detecting characteristics associated with writing quality, it evaluates writing proficiency and generates scores that may be utilized for both scoring and feedback. This technique is especially helpful for large-scale tests when objective and consistent grading is crucial.

4.3. Benefits of AI Grading Tools

- **Time-Saving**

Assessments can be processed and graded using time-saving AI grading tools far more quickly than by hand. This effectiveness enables teachers to give pupils quick feedback, which is essential for successful learning.

- **Consistency**
  AI systems provide uniform grading standards by applying the same criteria to every student input. This encourages impartiality in evaluation and lessens the variety that human graders may provide.
- **Scalability**
  AI grading technologies are perfect for large classes or universities with high enrolment rates since they can manage multiple evaluations at once. Regardless of the size of the class, this scalability guarantees that every student receives timely feedback.
- **Global Reach**

AI grading systems are available online, allowing educational institutions to administer tests and give students feedback from all over the world. Institutions that provide online courses or have overseas students will especially benefit from this.

4.4. Case Study: Gradescope's Application in STEM Courses at Duke University

To improve grading consistency and efficiency, Duke University has integrated Gradescope into its STEM classes. Students can retake tests and get the best mark by using Gradescope, which the university utilizes to give online exams. Students' learning outcomes have improved and their stress levels have decreased thanks to this method. Additionally, Gradescope has made grading easier, enabling teachers to give students timely and reliable feedback.

4.5. How Gradescope Changes Higher Education Grading Procedures

4.5.1. Simplified Administration of Assessments

With Gradescope, teachers may easily conduct a variety of tests, both in-person and online. This adaptability guarantees that teachers can select the approach that best suits their teaching situation, improving the quality of the learning process as a whole.

4.5.2. AI-Powered Efficiency Grading

Gradescope's AI-assisted grading capabilities are among its most notable features. By grouping comparable student comments using sophisticated algorithms, the platform enables professors to score several entries at once. This method guarantees uniformity in grading across sizable cohorts while simultaneously saving time.

4.5.3. Adaptable Rubrics for Regular Assessment

Teachers can design comprehensive rubrics that can be applied uniformly to all student submissions using Gradescope's dynamic rubric system. When grading complicated tasks, this function is very helpful because it guarantees that all students are assessed using the same standards.

4.5.4. All-inclusive Feedback Systems

Instructors can use the platform's capabilities to provide thorough comments on student submissions. By addressing particular areas for growth and promoting a more individualized learning experience, this feedback may be customized for each learner.

4.5.5. Learning Management System (LMS) Integration

An integrated teaching and learning environment is made possible by Gradescope's smooth integration with multiple LMS platforms. Through this interface, instructors can effectively administer their courses and students can readily access their grades and feedback.

4.6. Case Studies: Gradescope in Higher Education

4.6.1. Improving Big Lecture Classes at Indiana University

In order to investigate how teachers used Gradescope in large lecture sessions with more than 100 students, Indiana University carried out a qualitative, multi-case research. According to the results, Gradescope assisted teachers in overcoming the difficulties of consistently assigning grades, giving prompt feedback, and grading a high volume of assignments. Notably, when Gradescope was implemented during the semester, average course grades rose and course drop/fail/withdraw rates declined. Teachers reported better student satisfaction and more efficient grading.

4.6.2. University of Southern California: Lifelong Learning Personal Assistant

The PAL3 tool is an intelligent learning guide created by the University of Southern California to encourage lifelong learning. This project exemplifies the larger trend of incorporating AI to assist individual students throughout their academic journey, even if it has nothing to do with Gradescope. In order to identify learning gaps and suggest resources to support achieving learning objectives, PAL3 evaluates students' present knowledge and skill sets.

4.6.3. Dayton University: Making STEM Exams Easier

In order to solve the issues raised by generative AI, the University of Dayton investigated incorporating AI into

STEM courses at the lower and mid-level. The objective was to implement deliberate changes that support meaningful learning, academic integrity, and student development while acknowledging the existence of AI.

4.6.4. University of Manchester: Programming Assignment Auto-grading

Gradescope was used by the University of Manchester to make programming assignment auto-grading easier. Instructors configure scripts that run the supplied code, install required dependencies, and produce results that meet predetermined standards. Students' learning experience was improved by this method, which guaranteed a consistent setting for contributions and permitted varying degrees of visibility in feedback.

4.6.5. Gradescope's Use in STEM Courses at Duke University

Gradescope has played a significant role in improving the consistency and efficiency of grading at Duke University, especially in STEM courses. Exams are given online by the university using Gradescope, which enables students to repeat them and get the greatest mark. Students' learning outcomes have improved and their stress levels have decreased thanks to this method.

Additionally, Gradescope's adoption has expedited the grading process, enabling teachers to give students quick and reliable feedback. The benefits of Gradescope for teaching and learning in higher education are demonstrated in this case study.

4.6.6. Important Takeaways

- **Scalability in Large Classes**: Indiana University and other institutions have shown that Gradescope can efficiently handle grading in large lecture classes, enhancing productivity and student results.
- **AI Integration for Personalized Learning**: Resources such as USC's PAL3 demonstrate how AI may help with lifelong learning and customized learning pathways.
- **Adapting to Technological Changes**: In order to uphold academic integrity and promote worthwhile learning experiences, universities are investigating methods to incorporate AI into STEM courses.
- **Improving Programming Education:** One example of how AI may expedite coding tests and offer consistent feedback is the University of Manchester's use of Gradescope to automatically grade programming assignments.

In conclusion, by automating the grading process, offering consistent evaluations, and relieving teachers of the constraints associated with manual grading, artificial intelligence (AI) grading technologies are transforming the educational environment. This change is being spearheaded by tools like Gradescope, Turnitin's e-rater, and ETS's e-rater.

AI technology will probably become more integrated into educational evaluation procedures as it develops further, providing both teachers and students with even more advantages.

Gradescope is transforming higher education grading processes by offering resources that improve productivity, consistency, and feedback quality. Its AI-assisted grading, dynamic rubrics, and seamless connection with LMS systems make it a useful resource for educators, particularly in STEM disciplines. The encouraging results seen at universities like Duke University highlight Gradescope's potential to revolutionize higher education assessment procedures.

Chapter 5: AI-Powered Curriculum Development for Education's Future

Overview

Traditional educational paradigms are becoming less and less effective in a time of fast technological breakthroughs and changing labour market demands. *AI-driven curriculum design must be used by educational institutions to guarantee that students have the necessary abilities.* Utilizing performance analytics and labour market data, curriculum may be dynamically adjusted to meet industry demands, producing a workforce that is skilled and flexible.

5.1. Making Use of Performance Analytics and Labour Market Data

1. **Integration of Labour Market Data**

Real-time labour market data is now being used by educational institutions to guide the creation of curricula. Large datasets are analysed by platforms such as Coursera's talents Graph to determine the talents that are in demand across a range of businesses. For example, the 2025 Job abilities Report showed that learners' demand for generative AI abilities increased by an astounding 866% year over year, highlighting the need for curricula to change to meet this demand.

1. **Using Performance Analytics to Keep Improving**

Performance analytics are being used by institutions to track student development and pinpoint areas where the curriculum needs to be improved. Real-time modifications to learning pathways and content delivery are made possible by adaptive learning platforms, like those utilized at Arizona State University (ASU), which gather detailed data on student interactions.

5.2. Examples of AI-Powered Curriculum Development

5.2.1. The Skills Graph on Coursera

An AI-powered platform called Coursera's talents Graph connects talents to courses to give students individualized learning paths. The tool finds skill gaps and suggests relevant resources by examining learner behaviour and course material. This strategy guarantees that curriculum stay in line with changing industry demands.

5.2.2. Adaptive GenEd Courses at Arizona State University

The use of adaptive learning technologies in general education classes was first introduced by ASU. ASU created adaptive courseware in partnership with CogBooks for classes such as HIS 110 (U.S. History Since 1865) and BIO 100 (Introductory Biology). These courses have higher engagement and retention rates because they use real-time analytics to customize the curriculum to each student's needs.

5.3. Matching Industry Requirements with Curriculum

5.3.1. A. Curriculum Development That Is Dynamic

Institutions are implementing agile curriculum creation methodologies that integrate ongoing input from stakeholders in the business. Universities may make sure that their programs meet the needs of the workforce both now and in the future by forming advisory boards made up of professionals from the sector.

5.3.2. Cooperation with Business Partners

Collaborations between academic institutions and business executives make it easier to jointly develop courses that are both current and innovative. These partnerships frequently lead to the creation of specialized training programs that close the skills gap, internship possibilities, and cooperative research projects.

5.4. Prospects for AI-Powered Curriculum Development

5.4.1. A. Tailored Educational Routes

The development of highly customized learning experiences will be made possible by AI advancements. By evaluating individual learning styles, preferences, and progress, AI may offer individualized content and exams, optimizing the learning journey for each student.

5.4.2. Using Predictive Analytics to Align the Workforce

Future labour market trends will be predicted in large part by predictive analytics. AI can help guide curriculum changes that proactively address projected skill shortages in a range of industries by examining past data and new trends.

In conclusion, a paradigm change in education is represented by the incorporation of AI into curriculum design. Educational institutions can develop dynamic courses that not only satisfy present industry demands but also foresee future ones by utilizing labour market data and performance analytics. AI-driven strategies are opening the door to a more adaptable and successful educational environment, as evidenced by organizations like ASU and platforms like Coursera.

5.5. Using Labour Market Information to Develop Curriculum

5.5.1. Recognizing the Need for Skills

AI can determine the most in-demand talents by analysing large datasets from industry publications, job ads, and labour market trends.

For example:

- The Skills Graph on Coursera connects hundreds of skills from many industries to pertinent courses. It pinpoints learners' ability gaps and suggests focused learning paths.
- For instance, AI can suggest network security, cloud security, and ethical hacking courses if it notices a spike in the need for cybersecurity knowledge.

Establishing a direct link between education and the workforce guarantees that graduates are not just knowledgeable but also employable.

5.5.2. Making Use of Performance Analytics

In order to continuously improve the curriculum, performance analytics looks at learning behaviours, assessment outcomes, and student engagement:

- AI keeps note of which subjects students find difficult and which they pick up quickly.
- Real-time curriculum adaptation allows for the acceleration of advanced themes or reinforcement of weak areas.
- For instance, Arizona State University (ASU) gathers

information about how students interact in general education classes so that teachers can modify the course material and create individualized learning plans.

5.6. Curriculum Platforms Driven by AI

5.6.1. Skills Graph for Coursera

- An AI-powered platform that connects certifications and courses to talents.
- Based on their skill gaps and career objectives, learners receive tailored advice.
- Assists academic institutions and business training initiatives in creating curricula that meet industrial demands.

5.6.2. ASU's Adaptive Learning Systems

- General education (GenEd) courses like BIO 100 (Intro to Biology) and HIS 110 (U.S. History) are tailored to student performance using ASU's adaptive learning technology.
- While advanced learners can proceed, students who are having trouble understanding fundamental topics are given additional practice.
- **Result**: decreased course failure rates, enhanced retention, and increased engagement.

5.7. Matching Industry Requirements with Academic Programs

5.7.1. Curriculum Development That Is Dynamic

Universities can now regularly adjust their curriculum in response to changes in the labour market thanks to AI:

- Industry experts serve on advisory committees that examine and verify the curriculum's content.
- Employers and educational institutions maintain skill alignment through feedback loops.
- For instance, Georgia Institute of Technology updated its computer science curriculum in real time to include AI, machine learning, and data analytics by collaborating with prominent figures in the industry.

5.7.2. Industry Cooperation

- AI-guided courses incorporate project-based learning, co-ops, and internships.
- Collaborative studies and business-backed initiatives guarantee that students have pertinent practical experience.
    1. **Case Study: Adaptive GenEd Courses at Arizona State University (ASU)**

Leading the way in AI-powered curriculum creation is ASU:

- **Implementation:** To develop adaptive courseware for beginning courses, ASU collaborated with CogBooks.
- **Data Analytics:** AI monitors student development, spots gaps, and customizes lesson plans.
- **Outcomes:** Better learning outcomes, higher retention rates,

and enhanced student engagement.

- **Impact:** Students are better prepared for advanced coursework and industry-ready abilities thanks to a learning experience that is customized to their speed and comprehension level.

1. Prospects for AI-Powered Curriculum Development

1. Curriculum Predictive Modelling

Before there is a serious skills deficit, AI will predict new trends in the labour market and recommend changes to the curriculum. This guarantees that pupils are prepared for the future.

1. Tailored Educational Routes

Adaptive AI can suggest additional courses or micro-credentials to improve work preparedness. Students receive tailored content depending on their learning preferences, pace, and progress.

1. Integration of Lifelong Learning

AI-driven curriculum design ensures professionals to remain competitive throughout their careers by extending beyond formal education to up-skilling and reskilling platforms.

In conclusion, an innovative approach to education is represented by AI-driven curriculum design, which makes courses more dynamic, responsive, and in line with needs from the actual world.

- Tailored learning routes that optimize retention and engagement are advantageous to students.

- Businesses and educational institutions work together to guarantee that graduates have employable, future-ready skills.

AI makes sure that education changes with the workforce by utilizing performance analytics, labour market data, and adaptive technology, resulting in a system that is genuinely future-proof.

Chapter 6: IoT, Analytics, and Predictive Insights in Smart Classrooms

Overview

Chalkboards and dry lectures are no longer the norm in 21st-century classrooms. Classrooms are evolving into dynamic, interactive, and predictive learning environments as a result of the convergence of artificial intelligence (AI) and the internet of things (IoT). In addition to improving learning, these "smart classrooms" use data, connection, and clever algorithms to foresee problems before they become serious.

6.1. IoT and AI in Classrooms

The Internet of Things (IoT) is a network of interconnected gadgets that can exchange and gather data. These gadgets transform regular classrooms into dynamic learning spaces when paired with AI. Among the examples are:

6.1.1. **Smart Boards:** AI is integrated into contemporary interactive whiteboards, such as Google Jamboard or Promethean ActivPanel, to read handwriting, decipher diagrams, and even make real-time resource recommendations. For example, in a math class, the system can instantly offer suggestions or detailed corrections when a student solves a problem wrong.

6.1.2. **Smart Attendance Systems:** Attendance tracking is automated by IoT-enabled biometric scanners and facial recognition cameras. In addition to saving time, these systems give administrators and teachers access to real-time data that helps them spot tardiness or absenteeism trends. Students whose attendance patterns might suggest potential academic risk can subsequently be flagged by AI systems.

6.1.3. **Environmental Sensors:** Sensors that keep an eye on temperature, lighting, and air quality are installed in smart classrooms. AI examines these variables to maximize comfort and focus in the learning environment. For instance, research indicates that cognitive function is considerably diminished by CO_2 concentrations over 1,000 parts per million; IoT sensors can notify personnel to make proactive ventilation adjustments.

6.1.4. **Connected Learning Devices:** AR/VR headsets, tablets, and laptops gather usage data on student involvement. AI uses this data to modify how the curriculum is delivered, guaranteeing that students who have trouble with particular subjects get the help they need.

6.2. Predictive Analytics: Recognizing Students at Risk

Predictive analytics is one of AI's most revolutionary effects on smart classrooms. AI can detect students who are at risk of falling behind before they fail by evaluating past data as well as current inputs, such as attendance, assignment completion, participation, and test results:

- **Early Intervention:** AI is able to identify trends like low engagement, skipped assignments, or deteriorating grades. Teachers can respond to signals by offering adaptive learning modules, counselling, or tutoring.
- **Resource Allocation**: Schools are better able to distribute resources for support, like specialized education or peer mentorship.
- **Behavioural Insights:** Predictive analytics can identify kids who are displaying stress or disengagement, which enables counsellors to proactively address mental health issues outside of the classroom.
- **Example:** A student who struggles with algebra might regularly attend classes yet routinely receive below-average grades on assignments. Early detection of this tendency and tailored solutions like interactive problem-solving sessions, adaptive homework assignments, or peer cooperation are possible using AI-powered analytics.

6.3. Case Study: Georgia State University: Lowering Dropout Rates

A strong illustration of predictive analytics in operation can be seen at Georgia State University (GSU). Due to high first-year dropout rates, GSU put in place a predictive analytics system powered by AI that:

1. Gathered information from a variety of sources, such as attendance in class, financial aid status, academic achievement, and use of campus resources.
2. Before they failed any classes, students who were at risk of dropping out were identified.
3. Proactively alerted students and advisers, triggering actions like financial counselling, academic coaching, or individualized study plans.

Results: GSU decreased its total dropout rate by 21% in a short period of time, especially for historically underrepresented groups. Because students felt encouraged and guided rather than left to fend for themselves, the predictive analytics system also increased student happiness.

This example illustrates how AI- and IoT-powered smart classrooms can advance beyond reactive education, in which interventions take place only after failure, to proactive and predictive education, in which data informs choices that improve student results.

Diagram: Smart Classrooms – IoT, Analytics, and Predictive Insights

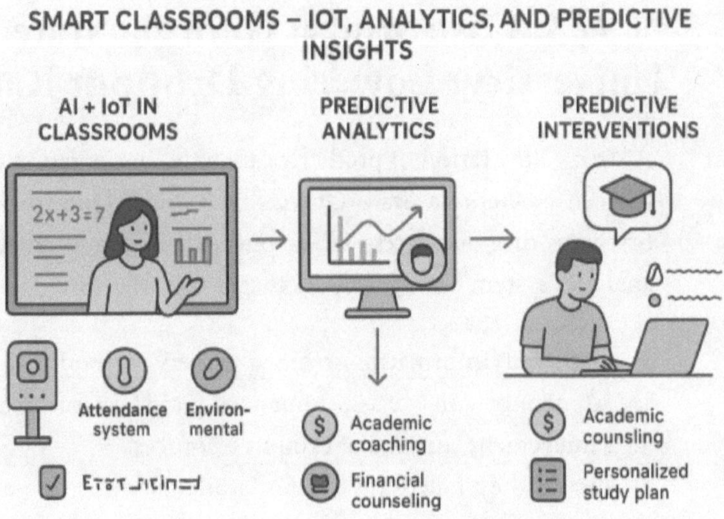

Figure 5: Smart Classrooms – IoT, Analytics, and Predictive Insights

In conclusion, dynamic, data-driven learning is replacing static instruction in smart classrooms. Teachers now have access to real-time data on student performance and engagement thanks to AI and IoT:

- Learning experiences are customized for each student based on their learning preferences and speed.
- Organizations are able to predict difficulties, distribute funds effectively, and lower dropout rates.

Future classrooms will be proactive, sympathetic, and responsive in addition to being intelligent. Education may finally transition from one-size-fits-all methods to really tailored and predictive learning experiences by utilizing technology and data.

Chapter 7: Gamification and AI: Learning Through Play

Overview

Textbooks, lectures, and standardized tests are no longer the only tools used in the classroom of the future. As digital natives who grew up clicking, swiping, and playing, Generation Z and Generation Alpha find "learning through play" to be a natural concept. Artificial Intelligence (AI)-driven gamification is revolutionizing education by fusing instruction and enjoyment. Students are more likely to participate, stick with, and succeed when learning feels like a game.

7.1. How AI Customizes Learning Games for Various Students

Learning became more enjoyable with traditional gamification (points, badges, leaderboards), but it was mainly "one-size-fits-all." By instantly adjusting games to each learner's requirements and preferences, artificial intelligence (AI) is already elevating gamification:

- **Adaptive Difficulty:**

AI dynamically modifies difficulty by examining a learner's progress, response time, and error patterns. To keep students interested, the game offers scaffolding if they have trouble understanding a concept and more difficult challenges if they perform well.

- **Personalized Feedback**:

AI-powered games offer context-aware recommendations that address particular errors in place of the standard "Try again," giving feedback that seems more like a coach than a critic.

- **Customization of the Learning Path**:

AI adjusts the tasks' order. To ensure efficiency and confidence growth, a student who struggles with fractions but excels in geometry, for instance, might be led along a different path than their peers.

- **Integration of Emotional Intelligence**:

Some sophisticated systems even use eye movement, click behaviour, or voice to monitor student participation (in VR/AR games). The game may enter a "mini-win mode" to boost morale before continuing if frustration is detected.

7.2. Examples of AI-Powered Gamified

7.2.1. Language Learning using Duolingo

The secret to Duolingo's worldwide success is the combination of gamification and AI. As they master new languages, learners compete on leaderboards, unlock streaks, and accrue XP points. Beneath the lighthearted façade, however, Duolingo's AI algorithms modify grammar and vocabulary tasks according to memory retention, fluency speed, and errors.

- Duolingo employs spaced repetition AI models to reintroduce a verb conjugation in various contexts until mastery is attained if a learner consistently forgets it.
- The program even identifies "drop-off points" for users, or places when students typically give up, and offers adaptive support, reminders, and streak prizes as motivational nudges.

7.2.2. **Math Adventure Prodigy**

Prodigy transforms math into a fantasy role-playing game in which students solve math problems to fight monsters. With reference to curriculum standards, AI makes sure that every battle corresponds to the learner's ability level:

- Teachers are given dashboards that display their personal strengths and shortcomings in real time.
- Why Math practice becomes ingrained and pleasurable as students who might otherwise shun math workbooks enthusiastically check in to "level up" their characters.

7.2.3. Classroom Engagement through Classcraft

The entire classroom setting is made more engaging using Classcraft. Students work in groups, accomplish tasks related to academic objectives, and receive points for good behaviour. Teachers can use AI to monitor participation trends and recommend engagement tactics to pupils who aren't interested.

7.2.4. Gamification as a Gen Z and Gen Alpha Motivator

- **Generation of Instant Feedback**: These generations are used to receiving likes, shares, and in-game awards instantly. This digital culture is reflected in AI-driven gamified learning, which provides instant feedback loops.
- **Collaboration and Competition**: Leaderboards, team challenges, and multiplayer learning missions promote constructive rivalry as well as cooperation.
- **Storytelling and Immersion:** Narrative-driven learning appeals to Gen Z and Alpha. AI is able to include personalized narratives into classes, transforming an arithmetic exercise into a puzzle-solving task or a history lecture into an adventure.
- **Micro-Learning Fit**: TikTok and Instagram have sculpted short attention spans, which are well suited for brief, gamified programs. AI guarantees the effectiveness of these micro-sessions.

7.2.5. **Case Study: AI-Powered Adaptation on Duolingo**

The development of Duolingo serves as an example of how AI and gamification can revolutionize education on a large scale:

- **Challenge:** After the first thrill wears off, a lot of language learners lose motivation. One of the biggest problems with e-learning is retention rates.

- **AI Solution:** A reinforcement learning AI model was launched by Duolingo, which forecasts when users are most likely to forget particular words or phrases. To improve long-term recall, these words are reintroduced right before memory deterioration.
- **Gamification Layer:** Leaderboards, jewels, and streaks motivate learners. Duolingo provides a "streak freeze" option for users who skip a day, striking a balance between forgiveness and motivation to lower dropout rates.
- **Outcomes:** Duolingo has more than 500 million users and daily engagement rates that are far higher than those of conventional e-learning platforms. Its success shows that gamification powered by AI is about maintaining long-term learning habits, not just having fun.

7.2.6. AI's And Gamified Learning's Future

Gamification will get even more immersive in the future:

- **AR/VR Classrooms:** Consider biology students playing a virtual frog dissection game in virtual reality where AI monitors their accuracy and offers in-the-moment guidance.
- **Neuro-Adaptive Gaming**: AI may soon be able to modify game complexity based on brainwave activity thanks to brain-computer connections, providing a learning environment that is precisely matched to cognitive load.
- **Global Access**: Playful education on inexpensive devices can be provided by AI-driven gamified platforms that scale to underprivileged communities.

7.2.7. **Important Takeaway:**

While AI makes sure that play is constant, productive, and tailored, gamification appeals to Gen Z and Alpha's innate play inclinations. The end effect is an educational system that inspires, engages, and turns students into lifelong learners and knowledge explorers.

Diagram: Gamification + AI in Global Education

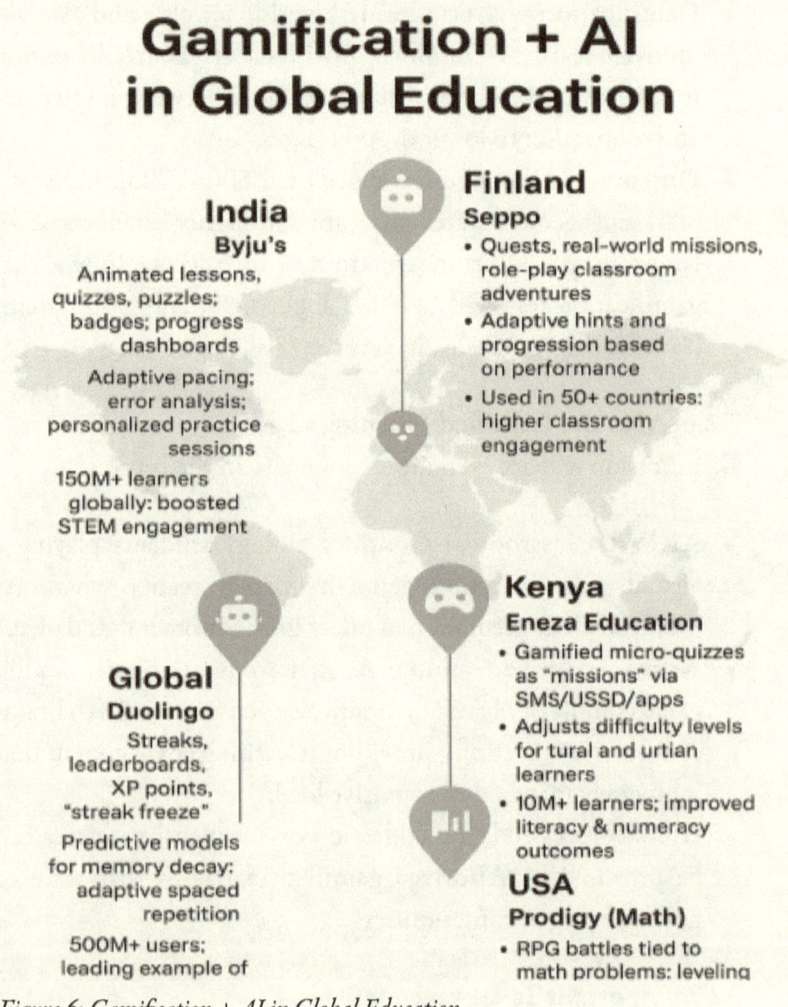

Figure 6: Gamification + AI in Global Education

7.3. Case Studies of AI-Powered Gamification Worldwide

7.3.1. **Case Study 1: Byju's (India) Edutainment's Ascent**

Through AI-powered gamification, Byju's, one of the biggest edtech platforms in India, has completely changed how millions of students interact with STEM courses.

- **Gamified Content**: Science and math classes are presented as interactive games, puzzles, and tests that frequently resemble mobile games more than traditional textbooks.
- **AI Personalization**: Byju's use adaptive algorithms to adjust the tempo of lessons based on learner success. The method offers prizes, game-like practice sessions, and educational animations to students who struggle with mathematics until confidence is established.
- Inspiring healthy rivalry in families and classrooms, students are given badges, points, and progress reports to share with their parents.
- **Impact:** Byju's has reached more than 150 million students worldwide, demonstrating the scalability of gamified AI teaching across socioeconomic backgrounds.

7.3.2. **Case Study 2: Game-Based Education in Actual Schools in Seppo, Finland**

Finland, a country renowned for its forward-thinking educational system, uses Seppo, a mobile game-based learning platform, to combine gamification and AI.

- **Interactive Missions:** Teachers design activities, challenges, and role-playing situations where kids learn by doing things in authentic settings (e.g., a math treasure hunt in the schoolyard or a history mission in a museum).

- **AI Support:** Seppo's system provides adaptive hints and progress based on choices while assessing student performance in real time.
- **Gen Z Engagement:** When lessons are designed as games, Finnish students report being more engaged. They feel more like engaged explorers than passive consumers.
- **Impact:** Finland's gamified AI approach is an exportable model for learning that is prepared for the future, since Seppo is currently utilized in more than 50 nations.

7.3.3. Case Study 3: Gamified Microlearning for Underserved Communities at Eneza Education (Kenya)

AI-powered gamification is assisting in closing the gap in Africa, where access to educators and textbooks might be restricted. Based in Kenya, Eneza Education offers affordable mobile-based instruction via apps, SMS, and USSD.

- **Gamified Learning Quests:** To motivate students to keep learning every day, they take brief tests that are presented as "missions" and receive points for completing them.
- **AI Personalization**: To ensure that rural students with limited resources receive the same individualized experience as urban learners, the platform adjusts the question complexity to the learner's level.
- **Scalability:** Proves gamified AI learning is not limited to affluent countries by functioning on even the most basic feature phones.
- **Impact:** Measurable gains in reading and numeracy results

have been achieved for over 10 million students in Kenya, Ghana, and Tanzania.

7.3.4. **Worldwide Viewpoint: Typical Threads**

Three motifs show up in Finland, Kenya, and India:

1. **Accessibility:** Gamified AI adjusts to local realities, whether it is through SMS-based missions in Kenya or high-tech VR in Finland.
2. **Personalization at Scale**: AI guarantees that each learner, irrespective of background, follows a customized route.
3. **Engagement Outside of the Classroom**: Gamification makes learning ongoing and self-directed by leveraging storytelling, competition, and curiosity.

7.3.5. **Important Takeaway:** AI and gamification are not just seen in affluent, city schools. The combination works everywhere, from smart schools in Finland to rural Kenya, meeting Gen Z and Gen Alpha where they are and how they learn best.

Diagram: Comparative Snapshot: Gamification + AI in Global Education

Country	Platform/ Example	Gamification Approach	AI Role	Impact/Reach
India	**Byju's**	Animated lessons, quizzes, puzzles, badges, progress dashboards	Adaptive pacing; error analysis; personalized practice sessions	150M+ learners globally; boosted STEM engagement
Finland	**Seppo**	Quests, real-world missions, role-play classroom adventures	Adaptive hints and progression based on performance	Used in 50+ countries; higher classroom engagement
Kenya	**Eneza Education**	Gamified micro-quizzes as "missions" via SMS/ USSD/apps	Adjusts difficulty levels for rural and urban learners	10M+ learners; improved literacy & numeracy outcomes
Global	**Duolingo**	Streaks, leaderboards, XP points, "streak freeze"	Predictive models for memory decay; adaptive spaced repetition	500M+ users; leading example of AI + gamification retention
North America	**Prodigy (Math)**	RPG battles tied to math problems; levelling up avatars	Maps student progress to curriculum standards; adjusts problem sets	Used in 150k+ schools; makes math practice addictive

Figure 7: Comparative Snapshot: Gamification + AI in Global Education

Chapter 8: Education for All: Inclusion and Accessibility

Overview

Beyond effectiveness, customization, and gamification, artificial intelligence (AI) has great promise for the educational sector. Fundamentally, AI may democratize education by guaranteeing that all students, irrespective of socioeconomic status, location, or handicap, have access to high-quality instruction. The goal of establishing a fair learning environment for everyone is around accessibility and inclusiveness, which are not ancillary advantages of AI.

8.1. The Way AI Helps Students with Disabilities

Accessibility technologies powered by AI are removing obstacles that have historically kept students with impairments out of regular educational settings. Through the use of computer vision, natural language processing, and predictive analytics, these tools enable students to engage with classmates on an equal basis.

3.4.1. **Speech Recognition:** AI-powered dictation tools can be used to translate spoken words into type for students with dysgraphia or movement disabilities.

For instance, students may compose essays, finish assignments, and even take part in conversations without typing thanks to Google Speech-to-Text and Dragon NaturallySpeaking, which offer real-time accuracy by adjusting to accents, speech patterns, and even contextual errors.

3.4.2. **Text-to-Speech (TTS):** TTS makes textual content accessible to students who are blind or have reading difficulties. For students with dyslexia, tools like Natural Reader or Read&Write highlight text as it is read out, strengthening word recognition; AI-powered TTS is now more human-like, lowering monotony and simplifying information.

3.4.3. **Visual Aids**

- AI computer vision tools help students who are blind or have low vision understand the visual environment.

- Microsoft Seeing AI uses a smartphone's camera to narrate text, identify items, recognize individuals, and describe scenes in real time.
- Similar to this, Google Lookout assists students with independent document reading, item identification, and classroom navigation.

3.4.4. Examples of AI Accessibility Tools

- **Microsoft Immersive Reader:** This program enhances reading comprehension by using graphic dictionaries, line focus, and text-to-speech. Particularly useful for ESL, dyslexic, and ADHD students.
- **Seeing AI (Microsoft):** This tool helps vision challenged students by reading workbooks aloud, recognizing classmates, and describing their environment.
- **Google Lookout:** This tool recognizes text, objects, and even cash in classrooms to provide audible feedback.
- **Be My Eyes (AI version):** Without requiring human volunteers, this technology uses AI to provide instantaneous answers to visual questions, such as explaining textbook illustrations.

3.4.5. Filling up the Gaps in Education in Under-Resourced Areas

Making sure that poverty and location are no longer obstacles to education is another aspect of accessibility, in addition to impairments. In areas with limited resources, AI is proven to be revolutionary.

- **Offline AI Tutors:** Programs such as Eneza Education (Kenya) reach students in remote locations without internet by using SMS and simple mobile phones to offer AI-driven courses.

- **Language Translation**: AI programs like Google Translate help multilingual classrooms by making sure students comprehend instruction in their mother tongues.
- **Predictive Analytics for Dropout Prevention**: To enable prompt interventions, NGOs employ AI to identify students who are at danger of dropping out of school.
- **AI Lessons Based on Audio and Radio**: These lessons translate text to locally relevant audio for students in low-literacy areas.

Diagram: AI for Accessibility and Inclusion Education for All

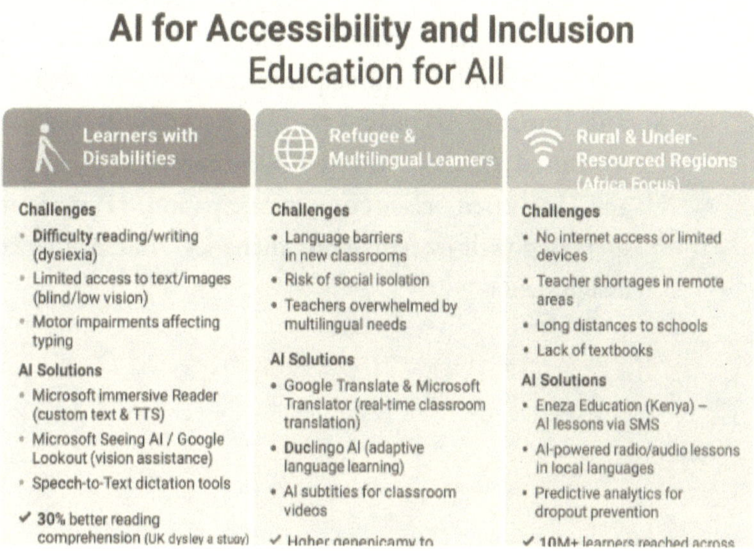

Figure 8: AI for Accessibility and Inclusion Education for All

3.5. Case Study 1: AI-Powered Resources Help Dyslexic Students Succeed

One in ten persons worldwide suffer from dyslexia, which frequently results in exclusion from text-heavy educational systems.

- **The Challenge:** Reading and writing difficulties lowered self-esteem, hindered development, and raised the likelihood of dropping out.
- **The AI Solution:** Microsoft Immersive Reader offered read-aloud capabilities and a customized text structure.
    - Better written expression was made possible by AI-powered grammar and spell-check tools.
    - Self-paced, visual-first learning was made possible by adaptive learning platforms.
- **The Impact:** According to UK research, dyslexic students who used AI demonstrated 30% improved comprehension and increased classroom participation. Parents noticed increased self-esteem and increased independence with assignments.

3.6. Case Study 2: AI-Powered Translation Resources Aiding Refugee Students' Adjustment to New Schools

Over 40 million children have been displaced by the worldwide refugee crisis, and many of them are now attending schools where the language spoken is foreign.

- **The Challenge:** Language problems frequently make it difficult for refugee students to assimilate, which results in social isolation, subpar academic performance, and increased dropout rates. Teachers struggle to offer tailored help since they are overburdened with multilingual classes.
- **The AI Solution:**
    - Textbooks and classroom instructions can be translated in real time using Google Translate and Microsoft Translator.
    - Children may learn new languages at their own pace with the aid of AI-powered language learning apps, such as Duolingo's adaptive AI.
    - Video courses with AI Speech-to-Text Subtitles instantaneously provide content in different languages.
- **The Impact:**
    - Using Microsoft Translator's classroom mode, which displays real-time subtitles on students' devices, refugee children from Syria and Afghanistan were able to follow lessons in Germany in a few of months.
    - Parents witnessed their children regain confidence and enthusiasm, lowering the chance of dropout; teachers reported more inclusive involvement in

discussions as students were able to express themselves in their home tongue while AI handled translation.

This example shows how, in international schools, AI is overcoming linguistic and cultural barriers in addition to aptitude gaps.

3.7. Case Study 3: Eneza Education, Kenya: AI Increasing Access in Rural Africa

Rural villages in many African nations lack internet access, infrastructure, and qualified educators. Millions of kids run the risk of falling behind just because they are unable to attend regular school.

- **The Challenge**: Students frequently travel great distances to attend schools in isolated Kenyan villages, where there are overcrowded classrooms and few resources. Internet-based learning systems are still out of reach, and many families cannot afford instructors or textbooks.
- **The Solution of AI:**
    - Eneza Education is a mobile learning platform powered by AI that uses SMS to deliver lessons to basic feature phones.
    - Students receive AI-generated explanations, tests, and progress feedback in addition to text questions in topics like science, math, and English.
    - Even in the absence of internet, the system creates a personalized learning path by adjusting difficulty levels to each learner's speed.
- **The Impact**:
    - Eneza has touched more than 10 million students in Ghana, Côte d'Ivoire, and Kenya.
    - Students who used Eneza demonstrated quantifiable gains in literacy and numeracy in areas with high dropout rates; parents report greater involvement since their children may learn safely from home, even in times of crisis like the COVID-19 pandemic.

This example demonstrates how AI may provide education for everyone, even in areas where traditional methods are insufficient, when it is localized and tailored to the conditions of low-resource contexts.

In conclusion, AI is changing the definition of accessibility in education, leading to more inclusive classrooms in the future. AI makes sure that learning is not a privilege for a select few but a right for everyone, whether it is helping a dyslexic child read fluently, assisting a blind learner in navigating the classroom, empowering a refugee student to overcome language difficulties, or sending a high-quality SMS education to a rural Kenyan youngster.

With the help of inclusive AI technology, the classroom of the future will be one in which no student is left behind and where access to high-quality education is no longer influenced by factors like geography, cultural background, or handicap.

Education for All, powered by AI inclusion, is the obvious objective.

Chapter 9: AI-Enhanced Immersion Learning through Virtual and Augmented Reality

Overview

Digital environments that allow students to enter a rainforest, explore the inside of a cell, or conduct a sophisticated surgery without ever leaving their desks are replacing static textbooks and chalkboards in the classroom of the twenty-first century. *Artificial Intelligence (AI)-enhanced Virtual Reality (VR) and Augmented Reality (AR) are not just "add-ons" to education; they are revolutionizing the way that knowledge is perceived.*

The unseen force underlying these immersive technologies is artificial intelligence. It guarantees that VR and AR environments instantly adjust to the behaviour, speed, and comprehension of students. When combined, they enable customized, interactive simulations that were previously only available in costly labs or dangerous real-world situations.

9.1. Opening Scenario: An Outside-the-Classroom Lesson

Despite the quiet in the classroom, each student is occupied with a chemistry experiment. Others take notes, one mixes chemicals, while another carefully modifies the flame of a Bunsen burner. However, there are no lab coats, test tubes, or beakers. Every pupil is donning a portable virtual reality headset.

The AI-powered technology in this virtual laboratory detects Sarah's hesitation when she is measuring a liquid. Her hand is guided and she is reminded of the proper measurement procedure by a virtual helper that instantly appears at her side. James inadvertently mixes two substances wrong across the room. The AI tutor gives him another opportunity to learn by pausing the simulation, explaining the mistake, and rewinding the experiment rather than allowing him to respond dangerously.

From a dashboard that shows real-time data, their teacher may observe who is doing well, who needs more practice, and which concepts are the most difficult.

This is not a dream of the future. Around the world, it is taking place in classrooms and institutions right now. AI-powered virtual and augmented reality is revolutionizing education by making every instruction immersive, flexible, and secure.

9.2. The Function of AI and VR/AR in Developing Interactive Simulations

Students may experience learning instead of merely absorbing it thanks to VR and AR:

- **Virtual Reality (VR):** Constructs entirely digital worlds. Students can perform virtual chemistry experiments, study historical events, or model actual workplaces.
- **Augmented Reality (AR):** Projects digital data onto the physical environment. Pupils can instantly view more information, 3D models, or explanations driven by artificial intelligence when they aim their tablets at a real object.

9.2.1. AI improves these by:

1. **Personalization**: AI systems monitor how well students are doing in simulations and modify the level of challenge. For instance, if a student is having trouble with titration in a virtual chemistry lab, the AI will slow down instructions and give specific tips.
2. **Real-Time Feedback**: Like a human teacher, AI-powered virtual reality tutors are able to examine a student's behaviour and instantly fix errors.
3. **Predictive Adaptation**: AI uses past performance to predict areas in which pupils could struggle and proactively modifies the situation to avoid failure and increase confidence.

Passive observation is changed into dynamic, interactive, and flexible learning experiences by this combination.

9.2.2. AI-Enhanced VR/AR in Education Examples

1. **Virtual Science Labs (Labster):** Students can conduct intricate experiments in immersive virtual labs provided by Labster without the need for expensive equipment or potentially dangerous ingredients.

- **AI Role:** Customizes difficulty levels, detects wrong steps, and offers adaptive advice.
- **Impact:** Students consistently and safely obtain real-world lab experience, which boosts their confidence and memory.

1. **ClassVR**: VR and AR headsets for schools are offered by ClassVR. Students can dissect virtual frogs, travel through ancient civilizations, or explore space.

- **AI Role:** Monitors student browsing patterns and modifies content to keep students interested. Better instructional support is made possible for teachers by providing them with analytics on student interaction.

1. **AI + AR Merge Cube**: Students can grasp an AR-enabled cube that allows them to visualize mathematical shapes and explore human anatomy. By customizing tests and assessments according to how successfully students engage with the digital models, AI improves the system.

9.2.3. AI-Enhanced VR/AR's Educational Benefits

1. **Safe Environments**

- Mistakes become teaching opportunities rather than expensive or potentially fatal mistakes;
- Students can practice emergency medical treatments or conduct risky experiments (such as combining volatile

chemicals) without risk.

1. **Scalable Access:**

- Not all schools have the funds for field trips or fully furnished labs. These experiences are widely available, irrespective of location or financial background, thanks to virtual labs and augmented reality modules.

1. **Memorable and Engaging Learning:**

- Experiential learning, which involves doing rather than reading, enhances memory, according to neuroscience research. AR and VR produce realistic, immersive memories that firmly establish information.

1. **Filling up the Equity Gaps**

- The educational playing field is levelled as students in underfunded schools have access to the same cutting-edge learning resources as those in prestigious universities.

9.2.4. Case Study: Medical Students Practice Surgeries using AI and VR

Medical students at Imperial College London are practicing complicated surgeries with VR headsets and AI-powered simulators:

- **The Problem**: Conventional surgical training is expensive, involves using live patients or cadavers, and puts students at significant danger. Errors can be lethal.
- **The Fix:** Students can enter a virtual surgery room using VR goggles. AI systems examine every motion, including the accuracy of an incision and the grip of a knife. With the help

of real-time feedback, posture, hand motion, and sequencing can be improved.

- **Result:** As a result of the immersive training, students who performed surgeries on actual patients felt less stressed because they had already "experienced" the scenario several times virtually. Students who trained with AI + VR also scored 30% higher in accuracy than those who trained solely with textbooks and lectures.
- **Scalability:** Unlike typical operating rooms, dozens of students can practice at once.

"It's like having a personal surgical mentor watching over your shoulder — but one that never gets tired," said a medical student.

9.2.5. Beyond Medicine: Broadening Perspectives

Although VR + AI has life-saving potential in medical, its applications are seen in all fields:

- **Engineering:** Before using actual materials, students can construct and test bridges in virtual reality.
- **History:** With the help of an AI teacher who narrates events, students can "walk" through ancient Rome.
- **Languages**: AI-powered virtual reality avatars mimic actual dialogues, assisting students in overcoming their nervousness when practicing speaking.
- **Environmental Studies**: To learn about biodiversity and the effects of climate change, students can immerse themselves in a coral reef or rainforest.

9.2.6. AI-Enhanced Immersion Learning's Future

Immersive Intelligent Learning is the new paradigm for education that is being hinted at by the convergence of AI, VR, and AR. In this model:

- In virtual reality classrooms, AI-powered adaptable avatars will serve as tutors.
- AI-generated holograms might be projected onto AR glasses to provide real-time concept explanations.
- On-demand access to cloud-based virtual reality labs will democratize access to higher education worldwide.

Future classrooms might be characterized by limitless digital environments where students are free to experiment, explore, and develop rather than by four walls.

Diagram: How AI Enhances VR / AR Learning

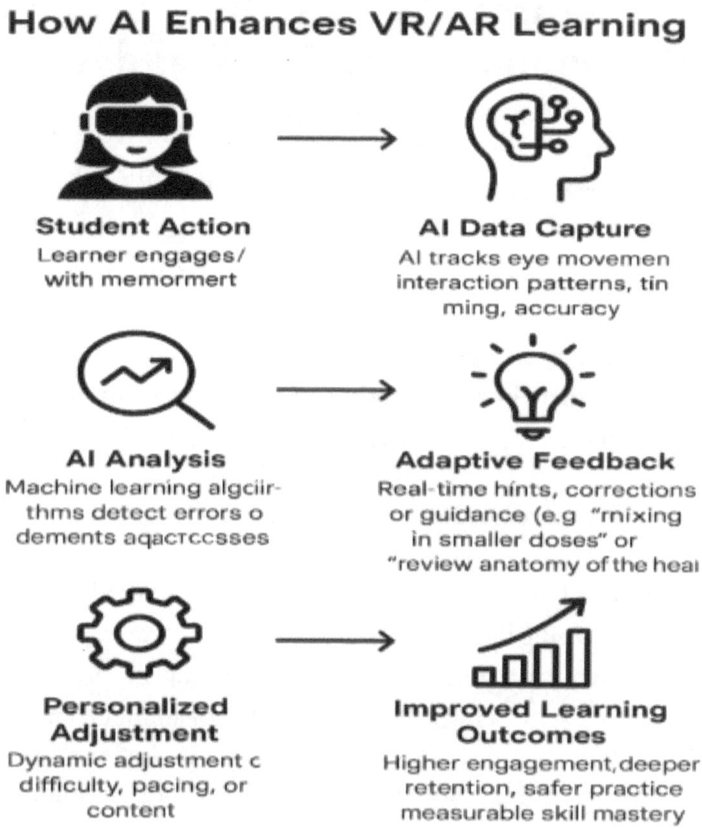

Figure 9: How AI Enhances VR / AR Learning

9.3. Future Prospects: The Upcoming Developments in AI, VR, and AR in Education

1. **By 2030 AI Teachers in Virtual Reality Classrooms**

Students will sit within a virtual space station under the guidance of an AI-powered hologram tutor rather than reading about Newton's laws. In addition to explaining physics, the tutor will modify gravity in real time so that students can experience the impacts of motion.

1. **AR Glasses As Daily Study Aids By 2032**

During class, AI-generated overlays will be visible to students using lightweight AR glasses. For instance, a typical classroom frog studying biology could "transform" into a real-time, semi-transparent 3D model with annotated parts.

1. **International VR Classrooms Without Boundaries by 2035**

VR and AI-powered translation will make classrooms truly global. An instructor in Japan, a student in Zambia, and classmates in Brazil will all be seated in the same virtual space, conversing in their original tongues while AI provides real-time translation.

1. **Neural-Linked VR Learning by 2040**

Students may "download" sophisticated abilities (such as engineering designs or surgical techniques) straight into their cognitive processes when brain-computer interfaces (BCIs) are included into virtual reality (VR). AI will monitor brain activity to find knowledge gaps and provide tailored immersive experiences to close them.

1. The Long View: Textbook-Free Education

Physical textbooks can completely vanish. Rather, AI-powered virtual reality environments will take the place of traditional textbooks, allowing students to live in the world rather than merely read about it.

9.4. Case Study: Using AR and AI to Introduce Science to Classrooms in Rural Areas

Many schools in rural Kenya lack completely functional science labs. Students have mostly used textbooks and chalkboard graphics to study chemistry, biology, and physics for decades, which has limited opportunities for experiential learning:

The Challenge:

- Students frequently performed worse on national scientific examinations as a result of a lack of practical experience;
- High student-teacher ratios made individualized instruction practically impossible;
- No access to lab equipment such as microscopes, chemicals, or models.

The Fix:

Low-cost AR-enabled smartphones and tablets with AI-powered learning apps were introduced by an NGO in collaboration with a local edtech business:

- By aiming their gadgets at a printed "marker card," students might initiate a 3D augmented reality simulation of a physics experiment, chemical process, or cell.
- AI examined every student's interaction, noting areas of difficulty, and provided in-the-moment guidance, adaptive tests, and further practice exercises.
- AI dashboards that summarized student performance were

given to teachers, assisting them in identifying pupils who required additional assistance.

Result:

The findings showed that science exam success rates increased by 22% in only a single year:

- Students expressed that they felt "as if the lab had come to them," which increased their self-assurance and passion for STEM.
- Teachers reported that by giving personalized feedback that they were unable to provide on their own, the AI-powered AR system assisted them in managing huge courses.

Important Takeaway: AI and AR are not limited to prestigious, high-tech institutions. It can close the resource gap by providing students in underprivileged areas with access to top-notch, immersive learning opportunities through reasonably priced devices and innovative content.

Diagram: Chapter Summary Table: AI + VR/AR in Education

Technology	Example	AI Role	Benefits
Virtual Science Labs (VR)	Labster	AI personalizes difficulty, provides real-time feedback on lab steps	Safe practice, repeatable experiments, affordable alternative to physical labs
VR Headsets for Classrooms	ClassVR	AI tracks engagement, adapts content, provides teacher analytics	Engaging experiences, immersive field trips, scalable for classrooms
Augmented Reality Objects	Merge Cube	AI tailors quizzes & interactive feedback based on student interactions	Hands-on 3D exploration, supports STEM visualization, boosts retention
Medical Training Simulators (VR + AI)	Imperial College London VR surgery training	AI analyses precision of movements, provides corrections & personalized feedback	Risk-free surgery practice, improves accuracy & confidence, scalable training
AR in Under-Resourced Schools	Rural Kenya AR science project	AI tracks learning gaps, adapts exercises, supports teachers with dashboards	Makes labs accessible, raises exam performance, bridges equity gaps

Figure 10: Summary Table: AI + VR/AR in Education

Note: With a balance of high-end and low-end use cases, this table provides you with an easy-to-read comparison of applications.

9.5. In summary: From Creativity to Learning

The concept of "learning by doing" is being redefined by the combination of artificial intelligence and virtual and augmented reality. Classrooms are becoming immersive environments free from physical constraints, allowing students to perform life-saving procedures, explore historical civilizations, and dissect cells without ever leaving their seats.

AI guarantees that these experiences are intelligent, individualized, and adaptive rather than one-size-fits-all. It turns VR and AR into living, breathing tutors by observing, learning, and guiding. This entails learning intricate processes with previously unheard-of accuracy for students at prestigious universities. It gives students in underdeveloped areas access to labs and experiences that they would not otherwise have.

AI-enhanced immersive learning holds great promise for engagement without limitations, scalability without inequality, and safety without sacrifice. Together, AI, VR, and AR are creating a future in which information is lived rather than observed by transforming imagination into reality and reality into a blank canvas for exploration.

One thing is evident as we look to the future: classrooms of the future will not be contained within walls, but will instead grow into limitless, sentient universes. Students who enter them will get more than simply knowledge; they will gain wisdom.

9.6. Questions for Thought and Discussion

1. **Immersion Capability:**

- *How might AI-enhanced VR and AR alter your own teaching or learning methods?*

- *What topic do you believe would gain the most from this change?*

1. **Educational Equity:**

- *How might immersive AI technologies aid in closing the gap between schools with enough resources and those with inadequate ones?*
- *What obstacles still exist?*

1. **Ethical Considerations:**

- *In delicate domains like medical education or historical simulations, what moral or security issues might emerge from the use of AI-powered VR/AR?*

1. **Teacher's Role:**

- *How do you anticipate the role of human teachers changing if AI tutors in virtual reality settings proliferate?*

1. **Looking Ahead:**

- *Let's say the year is 2040. With AI, VR, and AR completely incorporated into education, how might a normal school day look?*
- *How has it changed since today?*

1. **Practical Barriers:**

- *In your area or community, what monetary, technological, or cultural obstacles might impede the uptake of immersive AI-enhanced learning?*

1. **Engagement vs. Distraction:**

- *While VR and AR have the potential to enhance learning, they may also run the danger of diverting students' attention from more in-depth comprehension. How can teachers find the ideal balance?*

Important Takeaways

- AI, VR, and AR combine to provide intelligent simulations that change in real time, enhancing the hands-on, individualized, and captivating nature of learning.
- Examples such as Labster, ClassVR, and Merge Cube demonstrate how immersive technologies can make history, scientific labs, and difficult ideas come to life.
- Safety, scalability, and accessibility are advantages; students can practice risky tasks, schools can cut expenses, and underserved areas can obtain top-notch experiences

Case Studies Show The Impact:

- Using AI + VR surgery simulations, Imperial College London medical students increased their accuracy and confidence.
- With AI-powered AR laboratories, science exam scores in rural Kenyan schools increased by 22%.
- **The Future Is All-Encompassing**: Global VR classrooms and AI tutors have the potential to make education globally accessible, interactive, and borderless by 2035.
- In AI-driven environments, the function of the teacher will change from imparting knowledge to providing mentorship, guidance, and ethical oversight.

Chapter 10: AI Crossing Boundaries in Global Classrooms

Overview

Geography is no longer a barrier to education in the twenty-first century. Students from many nations, languages, and cultures can now easily learn together in classrooms that are becoming more global thanks to artificial intelligence. Language barriers are being broken, multilingual education is being supported, and cross-cultural cooperation is being promoted via AI-powered solutions. The way AI is turning the world into a school is examined in this chapter.

10.1. AI-Powered Multilingual Education and Translation

One of the largest obstacles to education has always been language. AI is currently breaking down this barrier by making multilingual education and real-time translation possible.

10.1.1. Important Innovations:

- **Real-Time Translation:** Learners can access content in their choice language thanks to AI's ability to translate lectures, written materials, and student interactions into numerous languages quickly.
- **Adaptive Language Support**: AI-powered tools are able to identify a learner's mother tongue and offer customized explanations or additional content.
- **Help with Pronunciation and Grammar**: AI-powered tools provide real-time feedback on syntax, semantics, and pronunciation, promoting language acquisition in addition to content comprehension.

10.1.2. Real-World Examples:

1. **Google Translate for Education:** This tool provides real-time translations into more than 100 languages for documents, webpages, and lesson content.

- Teachers can instantly deliver the same content to students in their local tongue by uploading syllabi or lecture slides in one language.

1. **Unbabel:** Produces excellent multilingual instructional resources by fusing AI and human post-editing.

- Gives teachers the ability to create discussion starters, assignments, and feedback that are appropriate for classes around the world.

10.2. Distance Education + Intercultural Cooperation

AI is making it possible for educators and students to work together in real time, anywhere in the world. AI-powered virtual classrooms are emerging as centres for intercultural education.

10.2.1. Important Attributes:

- **Intelligent Scheduling**: AI can optimize synchronous learning sessions across continents and account for time zones.
- **Cultural Context Adaptation:** AI systems are able to modify content samples such that they are appropriate for various student groups' cultural contexts.
- **Platforms for Collaborative Learning**: AI modifies multilingual discussion boards to guarantee that everyone can speak efficiently.
- Real-world examples include **Coursera** and **edX,** which use AI to translate subtitles automatically so that students throughout the world may follow lectures in the language of their choice.
- **Microsoft Teams + AI translation:** This feature enables real-time captioning and translation during meetings, facilitating international student collaboration on projects.

10.3. Case Study: Jordanian Refugee Students

Context: There are numerous refugees living in Jordan, and because of language issues, many of them have no access to formal schooling. AI-powered translation technologies were utilized in a 2023 effort to close these gaps.

Implementation: Using AI-powered translation systems, students participated in blended learning sessions where lecture contents were translated into Arabic, English, and French.

- AI chatbots provided pupils with immediate assistance in a variety of languages.
- To guarantee understanding, assignments and tests were translated automatically, negating the need for human translators.

Impact: Compared to traditional language instruction alone, students showed a 40% improvement in comprehension tests, and enrolment rates in refugee education programs rose by 35% in just six months.

- Instructors stated that AI technologies enabled them to concentrate on teaching instead of translating, resulting in more meaningful interactions with pupils.

Conclusions: This study demonstrates how artificial intelligence (AI) may turn classrooms into genuinely global settings, enabling access to top-notch education even for groups that face linguistic and cultural obstacles.

10.4. Global Classrooms' Future

AI-powered global classrooms promote equity, cooperation, and understanding between students in addition to translation:

- AI tutors for multilingual education: offering round-the-clock support in the native tongues of the pupils.
- Cultural exchange initiatives: AI can facilitate cooperative global efforts and model cross-cultural situations.
- Inclusive curriculum design: AI makes ensuring that learning materials are understandable and pertinent to a wide range of international students.

Key Takeaways:

- AI is removing barriers related to language and culture in education; adaptive learning tools and multilingual translation increase access for marginalized communities.
- AI-driven systems enable cross-cultural cooperation, creating a genuinely global educational experience.
- Practical uses, such as Jordanian refugee schooling, show how AI may revolutionize cross-border communication.

Chapter 11: Human Role in AI Education, Ethics, and Privacy

11.1. Hazards: Tech dependence, algorithmic bias, and data surveillance

11.1.1. Data Surveillance

Significant worries around data privacy and surveillance are brought up by the use of AI in education. In K–12 classrooms across the US, programs like Gaggle keep an eye on student communications for indications of cyberbullying, self-harm, and other dangers. Although the goal of these systems is to safeguard students, they also gather a great deal of personal information, which sparks discussions about how to strike a balance between privacy and safety.

11.1.2. Algorithmic Prejudice

The 2020 A-level grading controversy in the UK is a clear illustration of algorithmic bias in the classroom. Students were scored using an algorithm created by Ofqual, the UK's exam regulator, in response to COVID-19. The algorithm unintentionally penalized pupils from underprivileged families and smaller schools by modifying teacher-assessed grades based on past school performance. A policy adjustment followed public outcry after nearly 36% of A-level grades fell short of teachers' judgments.

11.1.3. Technology Dependency

Students' ability to think critically and solve problems can be weakened by an over-reliance on AI tools. For example, the employment of ChatGPT and other AI tools for assignments in Australian institutions has raised questions about academic integrity and degree devaluation. To overcome these obstacles, universities are now investigating safe evaluation techniques and degrees devoid of artificial intelligence.

11.2. The Human Factor: The Reasons Teachers Are Still Needed

Even with AI's advances, human educators still have unique traits. According to one study, artificial intelligence (AI) can help with education, but it cannot replace teachers' emotional intelligence, moral discernment, and individualized support. In areas where AI is currently lacking, such as critical thinking, creativity, and social-emotional abilities, teachers are essential.

Teachers in Minnesota are gradually incorporating ChatGPT and other AI tools to help with lesson planning and administrative duties. They stress the value of preserving human control in education, meanwhile, and are nonetheless concerned about the possibility of AI-assisted cheating.

11.3. Frameworks for Policies Required to Control AI in Schools

Comprehensive policy frameworks are necessary to guarantee the ethical integration of AI in education. When using AI, the U.S. Department of Education has released guidelines that place a strong emphasis on openness, prejudice reduction, and strong privacy safeguards. To protect student data and advance equity, these recommendations call for consistent monitoring and compliance with current legislation.

Institutions such as IIT Delhi in India have also set up committees to investigate the ethical application of AI in education. In order to promote openness and critical participation, they suggest updating plagiarism regulations, requiring disclosure of AI usage in academic work, and incorporating ethical AI instruction into curricula.

11.4. Case Study: The 2020 UK A-Level Grading Scandal

Widespread inequalities in the grading system used by Ofqual for GCSEs and A-levels caused a nationwide uproar in the UK in August 2020. *Nearly 36% of A-level marks were below teachers' assessments after the algorithm modified teacher-assessed grades based on past school performance data.* Allegations of systemic prejudice resulted from this approach's disproportionate impact on kids from underprivileged backgrounds and smaller institutions.

The UK government reversed its stance and went back to using teacher-assessed grades as a result of the outcry. The event made clear how important it is for AI systems employed in education to be open, equitable, and accountable. It emphasized the value of human supervision and the possible dangers of depending too much on algorithmic judgment in crucial educational tests.

In conclusion, even if AI has the potential to improve education, ethical issues, privacy protection, and the value of human teachers must all be taken into consideration. We can take use of AI while preserving the fairness and integrity of educational systems by putting strong legislative frameworks in place and keeping human monitoring in place.

Chapter 12: The Future of Education: Humans and Machines Co-Evolve

12.1. Vision of a Hybrid Teacher-AI Ecosystem

Imagine a classroom where AI systems and human teachers work together harmoniously, each enhancing the other's abilities. In this ecosystem, *teachers concentrate on mentoring, providing emotional support, and encouraging critical thinking, while AI takes care of repetitive jobs like grading and administrative work.* Through this collaboration, learning experiences may be tailored, with teachers offering the human touch necessary for holistic growth while AI adapts content to each student's needs.

Future classrooms are dynamic ecosystems where human teachers and artificial intelligence work together to optimize learning outcomes:

- **Personalized Learning Paths**: AI develops adaptive curriculum by analysing the learning styles, gaps, and strengths of each individual learner.

Example: A student who struggles with mathematics is given AI-generated exercises that target trouble areas, whereas a student who excels in geometry is given more difficult assignments.

- **Collaborative Teaching:** While AI manages administrative and analytical duties, teachers concentrate on mentorship, critical thinking, and socio-emotional development.

Example: AI can grade multiple-choice and short-answer tasks automatically, highlighting odd trends for teacher evaluation.

- **Engagement & Gamification:** Teachers encourage dialogue and introspection while AI incorporates interactive components like virtual reality simulations and gamified learning.

Example: In a virtual biology lab, teachers facilitate discussions about the moral ramifications of genetic engineering while students use virtual reality to investigate cellular processes.

12.2. AI as a Supplementary Teacher, Not a Substitute

AI is a supplement, not a replacement. It improves instruction without taking away the human element:

- **Real-Time Feedback & Tutoring**: AI can offer prompt clarifications or suggestions, allowing educators to concentrate on conceptual knowledge.

Example: When teachers conduct one-on-one mentoring sessions, platforms such as Carnegie Learning or Squirrel AI provide immediate math feedback.

- **Data-Driven Decision Making:** AI monitors student involvement, forecasts the likelihood of dropout, and suggests remedial measures.

Example: Georgia State University used predictive analytics to notify advisers of students who were having difficulties, resulting in a 21% decrease in dropout rates.

- **Ethical Considerations**: Human supervision guarantees that AI suggestions are impartial, equitable, and suitable for the given environment. Teachers use empathy while interpreting AI discoveries.

AI should not be seen as a substitute for teachers, but rather as an aid. AI, for example, may evaluate student performance data to find learning gaps so that teachers can quickly address them.

Additionally, AI can provide students with real-time feedback, freeing up professors' time for more dynamic and interesting exercises.

The human element will always be at the centre of education thanks to this cooperative approach.

12.3. Prospects for the Future: Lifelong Learning Partners, Global Learning Ecosystems, and AI Mentors

- **AI Mentors**: State-of-the-art AI systems will act as individualized mentors, helping students create goals, giving guidance, and offering advise throughout their academic path.
- **Global Learning Ecosystems:** AI will make it easier for people all over the world to access high-quality educational resources and experiences, enabling education to transcend national borders.
- **Lifetime Learning Companions**: AI will facilitate lifetime learning by adjusting to each person's unique interests and professional path, making education a continual process.

12.4. Case Study: Finland's AI Strategy: AI Literacy Integration into the National Curriculum

When it comes to using AI into education, **Finland** has led the way. The national AI plan places a strong emphasis on the value of AI literacy and seeks to give every student the knowledge and abilities necessary to comprehend and use AI technologies. This program consists of the following:

- **Curriculum Integration:** AI principles are integrated into a variety of topics to guarantee that students understand them contextually.
- **Teacher Training:** To effectively teach AI principles and integrate them into their teaching practices, educators get professional development.
- **Collaborative Projects:** To promote experiential learning, students work together to create AI-driven apps.

By ensuring that students are both creators and consumers of AI, this all-encompassing approach equips them for a world where AI will permeate every aspect of life.

12.5. Forecasts for the Future

- **AI Mentors:** Individual AI friends assist students with their studies, extracurricular activities, and job preparation.

Example, A mentor in AI would advise a student to look into coding projects related to their interest in climate science.

- **Global Learning Ecosystems**: Students have access to global interactive resources. AI facilitates cooperation, translates content, and adjusts to cultural situations.

Example: refugee kids in Jordan can participate in virtual STEM courses taught by Finnish teachers by utilizing AI-powered translation tools.

- **Lifelong Learning Companions:** AI provides recommendations for up-skilling while monitoring professional development and lifelong learning.

Example: An AI companion suggests to an engineer an online course on quantum computing based on past learning trends and changing industry trends.

12.6. Case Studies

12.6.1. Case Study 1: The National AI Strategy of Finland

Finland incorporates AI literacy throughout all educational levels and subjects:

- **Curriculum Integration:** Robotics projects, data ethics talks, and coding exercises are used to teach AI concepts.
- **Teacher Training**: To successfully integrate AI-assisted instruction, educators participate in workshops.
- **Student Projects**: Students create AI-powered applications that tackle social challenges, like environmental monitoring prediction tools.

12.6.2. Case Study 2: The Smart Education Ecosystem in Singapore

- **AI Tutors:** In large classes, AI tutors provide individualized language and math education to support human teachers.
- **Smart Classrooms**: Analytics and sensors track student participation and make real-time pedagogical recommendations.
- **Result:** Better test scores and more engagement, especially in big, diverse classrooms.

12.6.3. Case Study 3: Microsoft + AI for Accessibility in the United States

- **Assistive AI Tools**: AI-powered reading and comprehension aids are used by students who have visual impairments or dyslexia.
- **Teacher Role**: Instructors use these resources into their class plans, emphasizing critical thinking and comprehension above memorization.
- **Result:** While promoting independence, students get learning results on par with their peers.

12.7. Final Thoughts: The Mind-set of Co-Evolution

- Teachers become into mentors, advisors, and moral supervisors.
  AI develops become context-aware, individualized co-teachers.
- By fostering fairness, participation, and lifelong learning, this hybrid model makes sure that education stays up with societal and technological advancements.

12.8. Important Questions Regarding AI in Education

We encourage everyone in the ecosystem to spend more time considering the following questions as leaders in pre-service and post-service teacher education, together with legislators, developers, and researchers, consider how AI may enhance teaching:

- *Does artificial intelligence raise the standard of a teacher's daily work? Are educators feeling less overburdened and better equipped to concentrate and instruct their students?*
- *Do educators have control over the AI tools that are employed with their students? Are they exerting control over the proper or improper use of AI-enabled tools and systems, allowing these tools and systems to make decisions for them?*
- *To what degree can educators use their voices and decision-making to enhance cultural responsiveness, decrease bias, and promote fairness while utilizing AI-enabled tools and systems?*
- *Are we avoiding the transfer of extra workloads or new duties to teachers in a way that counteracts the potential advantages of AI, even as it lessens one kind of teaching burden?*
- *Does the use of AI in the classroom give teachers greater in-depth knowledge about their students' strengths while maintaining their privacy?*
- *Are there sufficient safeguards against spying when AI systems are being utilized to assist teachers or improve instruction?*

Diagram: The Future of Teaching – Humans and Machines Co-Evolving

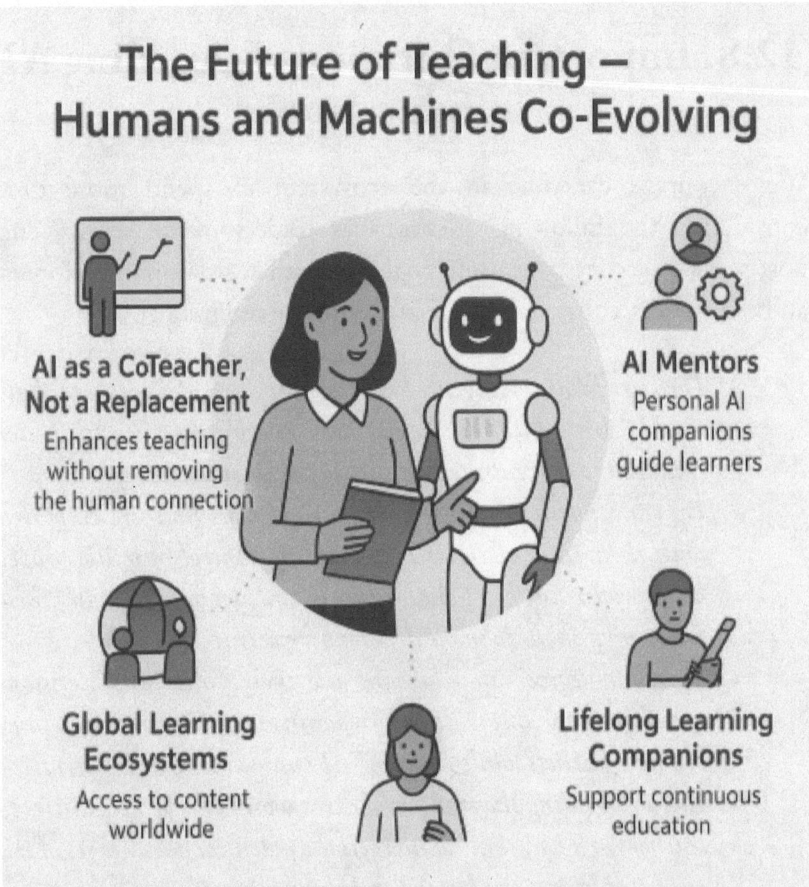

Figure 11: The Future of Teaching – Humans and Machines Co-Evolving

Conclusion: Teaching the Machines to Teach

As we come to the end of this investigation of AI in education, it is critical to consider the revolutionary ideas that have surfaced and to look ahead. The transition from conventional classrooms to AI-enhanced learning environments involves more than just a change in technology; it involves a fundamental rethinking of the role of the teacher, the experience of the student, and the distribution of information in society.

Important Themes Review

1. **From Providing Content to Facilitating Knowledge**

A recurring theme across the chapters is that AI is changing the definition of teaching. Education is no longer solely about imparting knowledge in a linear, one-size-fits-all fashion. AI turns the teacher into a knowledge facilitator by enabling individualized, adaptive learning. With the help of sophisticated tools that offer real-time insights on students' development, teachers are becoming into curators, mentors, and guides.

Example: AI algorithms evaluate students' real-time arithmetic problem-solving techniques in adaptive learning platforms such as **DreamBox Learning**. Teachers can transform passive learners into active participants by providing targeted assistance, posing challenging questions, and promoting strategic thinking, as opposed to concentrating only on providing the right answer.

1. **Humans and Machines' Coevolution**

AI exists to enhance human potential, not to replace teachers. Examples of AI systems functioning as co-teachers have been presented throughout this book, giving pupils scaffolding while allowing teachers to concentrate on tasks requiring creativity, interpersonal interaction, and critical thinking.

Case Study: **Finland's AI literacy program** incorporates AI tools into the national curriculum to help students learn computational thinking and problem-solving skills while providing teachers with analytics on student learning trends. Teachers can effectively co-evolve with the AI systems by designing lessons based on actionable findings.

1. **Global Learning, Accessibility, and Equity**

Additionally, AI could democratize education. Intelligent technologies are filling the gaps that have historically restricted access to high-quality education, from offering adaptive tools for students with disabilities to translating languages and giving text-to-speech.

Example: Seeing AI, a Microsoft product designed for students with visual impairments, transforms the environment into spoken descriptions so that students can interact with the contents on their own. In a similar vein, AI-powered translation platforms such as Unbabel enable intercultural cooperation, enabling refugee students in Jordan to study with classmates from around the world.

Getting Ready for the Classroom Driven by AI

The world of the AI-enhanced classroom is one of opportunity, accountability, and vision. The following players need to be aggressive in order to realize its full potential:

1. Instead of viewing AI as a danger, **Educators** ought to welcome it as a cooperative partner. Programs for professional development ought to emphasize:

- Deciphering insights from AI.
- Creating individualized educational programs.
- Preserving the human element, which technology cannot replace.

1. To guarantee the ethical, egalitarian, and successful implementation of AI in schools, **Policymakers** must develop frameworks. This covers:

- Controlling algorithmic bias and data privacy.
- Providing the infrastructure needed for AI implementation in schools with limited funding.
- Promoting studies on the long-term effects of AI on educational results.

1. In addition to traditional literacy, **Learners** must acquire AI literacy. To be competent in the twenty-first century, one must comprehend the limitations of AI tools, how they operate, and how to interact critically with content that has been curated by AI.

An Urgent Appeal

The use of AI in education is not just a pipe dream; it is already taking shape in classrooms all around the world. The main takeaway from our conclusion is unmistakable: we are educating machines to teach, not only students. Success in this day and age hinges on our readiness to accept change with consideration:

- Teachers must assume their responsibilities as knowledge facilitators and co-creators, and policymakers must develop inclusive, progressive legislation.
- Students need to take an active role in influencing the direction of AI-driven education.
- AI has the potential to enhance learning, but only if humans use it with intention, morality, and originality.

Reimagining education for a future in which humans and machines learn, develop, and teach together is an enormous problem as well as an unparalleled opportunity.

In conclusion, education is evolving, though not in the manner that many had anticipated. The classroom of the future is not one with automated lectures and quiet displays. In this dynamic ecology, machines and humans evolve, learn, and teach one another.

Fundamentally, AI is changing the function of the teacher from imparting knowledge to facilitating it. With AI acting as a co-teacher to increase their reach and insight, educators no longer merely impart knowledge; instead, they curate, mentor, and inspire. This is aptly demonstrated by platforms such as DreamBox Learning, where professors step in when curiosity, creativity, and critical thinking are most needed, while AI tracks each student's route toward problem-solving. The human touch is more important than ever in this situation.

But AI's promise is not just personalization—it is equity. Students with disabilities or linguistic difficulties can now fully engage in international learning networks thanks to tools like Seeing AI and AI-driven translators. From AI literacy initiatives in Finland to refugee classrooms in Jordan, the message is unmistakable: education becomes truly inclusive when people and robots work together.

However, learning cannot be transformed by technology alone. AI must be welcomed by educators as a collaborator, not a substitute. Adoption must be morally just, equitable, and easily available. In order to understand about AI—its advantages, disadvantages, and contribution to knowledge—students must acquire AI literacy.

We are training robots to teach, and in the process, we are educating ourselves to teach more effectively. This is an important demand. Although the AI-enhanced classroom will push boundaries, encourage innovation, and open up new possibilities, it will never fully replace the human element that gives learning purpose.

Education in this new age is about co-creating the future, not about forecasting it. Teachers, students, and machines are at the cusp of a once-in-a-lifetime opportunity: creating a world in which learning is unrestricted, knowledge is freely exchanged, and every student has the potential to succeed.

The question is whether AI can teach anymore. *How will we educate AI to teach? is the question. How will we improve as teachers as a result of this?*

Food for Thought....

Training students is no longer the only goal of education; we are also training machines to teach, and so teaching ourselves what it is to lead, inspire, and learn. Knowledge in AI-enhanced classrooms comes from a dynamic collaboration between machine intelligence and human intuition rather than from a single source.

Machines expand possibilities beyond our wildest dreams, educators become mentors and curators, and students become active co-creators. Education in the future will be more than just digital; it will involve people and technology working together to learn, develop, and create.

We are confronted with a pressing and significant question: *how will we mold this collaboration, and what sort of students—and educators—will we become?* — Patrick Mukosha.

Table of Figures

Bibliography

1. Griffiths, Dai; Frías-Martínez, Enrique; Tlili, Ahmed; Burgos, Daniel (2024). "A Cybernetic Perspective on Generative AI in Education: From Transmission to Coordination"[1]. International Journal of Interactive Multimedia and Artificial Intelligence. **8** *(5): 15. doi[2]:10.9781/ijimai.2024.02.008[3]. ISSN[4] 1989-1660[5].*

2. Rosemary Luckin, Kenneth R. Koedinger, Jim E. Greer; (2007), "Artificial Intelligence in Education: Building Technology Rich Learning Context That Work"; IOS Press

3. Shegquan Yu & Yu Lu;(2021), " An Introduction to Artificial Intelligence in Education (Bridging Human and Machine: Future Education with Intelligence)

4. Ouyang, Fan; Jiao, Pengcheng (2021-01-01). "Artificial intelligence in education: The three paradigms"[6]. Computers and Education: Artificial Intelligence. **2** *100020. doi[7]:10.1016/j.caeai.2021.100020[8]. ISSN[9] 2666-920X[10].*

---

1. *https://www.ijimai.org/journal/bibcite/reference/3430*
2. *https://en.wikipedia.org/wiki/Doi_(identifier)*
3. *https://doi.org/10.9781%2Fijimai.2024.02.008*
4. *https://en.wikipedia.org/wiki/ISSN_(identifier)*
5. *https://search.worldcat.org/issn/1989-1660*
6. *https://doi.org/10.1016%2Fj.caeai.2021.100020*
7. *https://en.wikipedia.org/wiki/Doi_(identifier)*
8. *https://doi.org/10.1016%2Fj.caeai.2021.100020*
9. *https://en.wikipedia.org/wiki/ISSN_(identifier)*
10. *https://search.worldcat.org/issn/2666-920X*

5. Selwyn, Neil (2022), "The Future of AI in Education: Some Cautionary Notes", European Journal of Education, 57(4): 620-631, ISSN 1465-3435

6. Hamilton, Llaa (2023-12-05). "Artificial Intelligence in Education: Teachers' Opinion on AI in the Classroom", Forbes Advisor. Retrieved 2025-07-15

7. Doroudi, Shayan (2023-12-01). "The Intertwined Histories of Artificial Intelligence and Education"[11]. International Journal of Artificial Intelligence in Education. ***33*** *(4): 885–928. doi[12]:10.1007/s40593-022-00313-2[13]. ISSN[14] 1560-4306[15].*

8. Thompson, David (2019-12-09). "Histories of Artificial Intelligence: A Genealogy of Power"[16]. www.hps.cam.ac.uk. Retrieved 2025-07-15.

9. Moor, James (2006-12-15). "The Dartmouth College Artificial Intelligence Conference: The Next Fifty Years"[17]. AI Magazine. ***27*** *(4): 87. doi[18]:10.1609/aimag.v27i4.1911[19]. ISSN[20] 2371-9621[21].*

---

11. https://doi.org/10.1007%2Fs40593-022-00313-2

12. https://en.wikipedia.org/wiki/Doi_(identifier)

13. https://doi.org/10.1007%2Fs40593-022-00313-2

14. https://en.wikipedia.org/wiki/ISSN_(identifier)

15. https://search.worldcat.org/issn/1560-4306

16. https://www.hps.cam.ac.uk/research/projects/histories-of-ai

17. https://ojs.aaai.org/aimagazine/index.php/aimagazine/article/view/1911

18. https://en.wikipedia.org/wiki/Doi_(identifier)

19. https://doi.org/10.1609%2Faimag.v27i4.1911

20. https://en.wikipedia.org/wiki/ISSN_(identifier)

21. https://search.worldcat.org/issn/2371-9621

10. Watermeyer, Richard; Lanclos, Donna; Phipps, Lawrie; Shapiro, Hanne; Guizzo, Danielle; Knight, Cathryn (2024-12-03). "Academics' Weak(ening) Resistance to Generative AI: The Cause and Cost of Prestige?"[22]. Postdigital Science and Education. doi[23]:10.1007/s42438-024-00524-x[24]. ISSN[25] 2524-4868[26].

11. *Eynon, Rebecca; Young, Erin (January 2021). "Methodology, Legend, and Rhetoric: The Constructions of AI by Academia, Industry, and Policy Groups for Lifelong Learning". Science, Technology, & Human Values.* **46** *(1): 166–191. doi[27]:10.1177/0162243920906475[28]. ISSN[29] 0162-2439[30].*

22. *https://doi.org/10.1007%2Fs42438-024-00524-x*

23. *https://en.wikipedia.org/wiki/Doi_(identifier)*

24. *https://doi.org/10.1007%2Fs42438-024-00524-x*

25. *https://en.wikipedia.org/wiki/ISSN_(identifier)*

26. *https://search.worldcat.org/issn/2524-4868*

27. *https://en.wikipedia.org/wiki/Doi_(identifier)*

28. *https://doi.org/10.1177%2F0162243920906475*

29. *https://en.wikipedia.org/wiki/ISSN_(identifier)*

30. *https://search.worldcat.org/issn/0162-2439*

Don't miss out!

Visit the website below and you can sign up to receive emails whenever Patrick Mukosha publishes a new book. There's no charge and no obligation.

https://books2read.com/r/B-A-HJNZ-POKWG

Did you love *AI in Education: Teaching the Machines to Teach*? Then you should read *AI in Agriculture: Farming the Future*[31] by Patrick Mukosha!

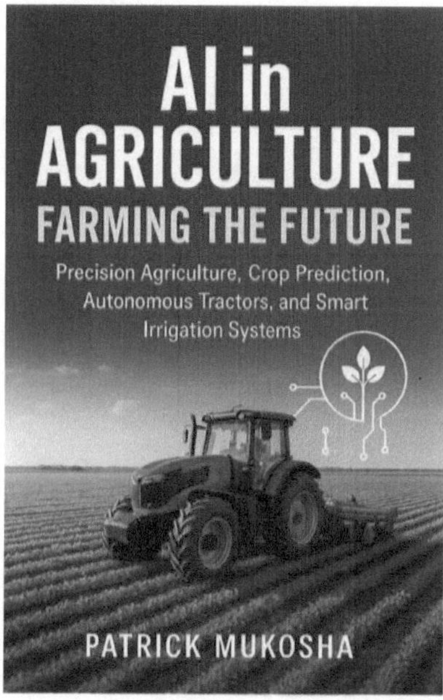

[32]

The book *explores the economic, environmental, and social effects of AI-powered farming in addition to the technology, drawing on the most recent worldwide research, real-world case studies, and future-focused scenarios.* In addition to addressing the issues of data ethics, farmer training, and fair access to technology, it tackles the promise of increased yields, decreased waste, and sustainable resource usage.

AI in Agriculture: Farming the Future presents a convincing picture of how humanity can use AI to feed a growing population, fight climate change, and develop a more intelligent, environmentally friendly, and resilient agricultural system, regardless of whether you

---

31. https://books2read.com/u/mdOzNX

32. https://books2read.com/u/mdOzNX

are a policymaker, agricultural entrepreneur, tech innovator, or just an interested reader.

"The future of farming is not just in the fields—it's in the Algorithms." - Patrick Mukosha

Also by Patrick Mukosha

GoodMan

Resilient Strategies: Thriving in Harsh Business Conditions
Strategic Entrepreneurship: Navigating The Path To Success
Decisive Power: Navigating How to Make Toughest Decisions
"Reigning the Boardroom: A Trailblazing Guide to Corporate Governance Success"
Fortifying Digital Fortress: A Comprehensive Guide to Information Systems Security
“Unleashing the Power of Inclusive Innovation: Transforming the World for All”
“Exploring Computer Systems: From Fundamentals to Advanced Concepts”
“Computer Viruses Unveiled: Types, Trends and Mitigation Strategies”
"The Pinnacle of Success: Unveiling the World's 20 Most Successful Brands in 2023”
“Mastering Relational Databases: From Fundamentals to Advanced Concepts”
“Navigating Change: A Comprehensive Guide to Change Management”
“Information Systems Unraveled: Exploring the Core Concepts”
"Careers in Information Technology: Network Engineer"

“Careers in Information Technology: Network and Systems Administrator”
“Careers in Information Technology: Database Administrator”
"Careers in Information Technology: Cybersecurity Analyst"
“Careers in Information Technology: Cloud Security Specialist”
"Careers in Information Technology: Blockchain Developer"
"Careers in Information Technology: DevOps Engineer"
"Careers in Information Technology: Quality Assurance Analyst"
"Careers in Information Technology: Machine Learning Engineer"
"Careers in Information Technology: Artificial Intelligence (AI) Engineer"
"Careers in Information Technology: Internet of Things (IoT) Developer"
"Careers in Information Technology: AR/VR Developer"
“Careers in Information Technology: IoT Embedded Systems Designer”
“Careers in Information Technology: Artificial Intelligence (AI) Robotics Engineer”
“Careers in Information Technology: IoT Solutions Engineer”
“Careers in Information Technology: Data Scientist”
"Careers in Information Technology: Computer Vision Engineer"
"The Sociology of Information Technology"
“Smart Cities: The Technology Transforming Urban Living”
"The Future of Connectivity: Unleashing the Power of 5G and Beyond"
" Cybersecurity 2030 - Strategies for a Secure Digital Future"
The AI-Human Merger: Becoming Super-Intelligent Beings
AI Unleashed: The Future of Artificial Intelligence and Human Evolution
The Digital Prophet: Predicting the Next Decade of Disruption
AI in Agriculture: Farming the Future
AI in Education: Teaching the Machines to Teach

About the Author

Patrick Mukosha is an ICT & Management Consultant. With 15+ years of IT experience, he's passionate about all things ICT. He also loves to bring ICT down to a level that everyone can understand. His works have been quoted on Academia by Researchers and ICT Practitioners (www.academia.edu). He has a PHD and MBA from AIU, USA, BSc(Hons) ICT, UEA, UK, Dipl, CCT, UK. He's a founder of PatWest Technologies.

About the Publisher

Patrick Mukosha is an experienced ICT & Management Consultant. With 15+ years of IT and Management experience. He's passionate about all things IT & Management. He also loves to bring IT & Management issues down to a level that everyone can understand. His works have been widely quoted by Researchers and IT Practitioners. He has a PHD and MBA from AIU, USA; BSc(Hons) ICT, UEA, UK; Dipl, CCT, UK. He's a founder of PatWest Technologies.

www.ingramcontent.com/pod-product-compliance
Lightning Source LLC
LaVergne TN
LVHW090405210926
848480LV00002B/463
* 9 7 9 8 2 3 2 5 5 0 6 7 7 *